The Modern Medical Student Manual

Learn faster, find fulfilling work and make ... edicine

By

Copyright © 2017/2018/2019/2020 by Chris Lovejoy.

All rights reserved.

No part of this publication may be reproduced, distributed, or transmitted in any form or by any means, including photocopying, recording, or other electronic or mechanical methods, without the prior written permission of the publisher, except in the case of brief quotations embodied in critical reviews and certain other non-commercial uses permitted by copyright law.

For information about permission to reproduce selections from this book, write to editor@medicalstudentmanual.com.

ISBN 9781973413592

www.medicalstudentmanual.com

10% of all profits from this book will go to the Against Malaria Foundation and the Schistosomiasis Control Initiative – two of the charities with the highest lives saved per cost.

Dedicated to Katherine

Contents

INTRODUCTION: FROM THAT DAY TO THIS BOOK 1

CHAPTER 1: MEDICINE FROM FIFTY THOUSAND FEET: PERSPECTIVE, TARGETS AND LIMITS 5
    FOLLOW THE TRAIL OF WHYS 7
    ATTEND YOUR OWN FUNERAL 10
    SET LIMITS, NOT JUST TARGETS 13

CHAPTER 2: THE FUNDAMENTALS OF FAST LEARNING 15
    SPACED REPETITION 17
    LEARN FOR UNDERSTANDING 21
    CREATE CONDITIONS FOR DEEP WORK 28
    FACILITATE CONTINUAL IMPROVEMENT 33

CHAPTER 3: MASTERING CLINICAL MEDICINE 39
    MAKING THE MOST OF CLINICAL TIME 41
    DECONSTRUCTING CLINICAL SKILLS 45
    MASTERING THE PHYSICAL EXAMINATION 47

CHAPTER 4: MAKE YOUR MARK ON THE MEDICAL FIELD (AND THE POWER OF SELF-EDUCATION) 57
    WHY SHOULD WE DO MORE? 58
    HOW CAN WE INCREASE OUR IMPACT? 61
    SELF-EDUCATION: THE 21ST CENTURY SUPER-POWER 65
    DEVELOPING FUNDAMENTAL TRANSFERRABLE SKILLS 69

CHAPTER 5: A SCIENTIFIC APPROACH TO RESEARCH 73
    DO YOUR OWN WORK 74
    THE IDEA 75
    THE SUPERVISOR 81
    WRITING THE PAPER 84

CHAPTER 6: COMMANDING CLEARER COMMUNICATION 87
    ORAL COMMUNICATION IN HEALTHCARE 88
    LEARNING TO TEACH WELL 92
    LEARNING TO WRITE WELL 94

IS MEDICINE RIGHT FOR ME? 101

IF MEDICINE GETS YOU DOWN 105

MEMORISATION TECHNIQUES 113

LEARNING FROM OTHERS 121

CONCLUSION 125

EPILOGUE 127

ABOUT THE AUTHOR 129

Introduction: From That Day to This Book

"I'll be there in five minutes", I said. I hung-up the phone and my heart skipped a beat.

Around me, it was just another day. A group of people were waiting at a near-by bus stop. Others were moving in all directions. On the surface everything seemed normal, but for me this was going to be a day like no other.

I turned and starting walking down the busy high-street, past the library and the bank and the café. I walked past the fish and chip shop, to which I had donated most of my pocket money over the years. A whiff of scampi made my stomach groan. But I had higher priorities right now.

I reached the final corner and turned. There was the car in front of me. I strode over, opened the passenger door and sat down. My mum was in the driver's seat. I tried to read her facial expression. It seemed reserved, perhaps deliberately so, but I couldn't trust my intuition. I needed to see it.

She handed me the white A4 envelope with a red shield stamped in the top right-hand corner. I saw it trembling slightly in my hands. For what felt like an age, I fumbled to open it. I grabbed its contents between my thumb and forefinger and freed it from the envelope.

Two seconds passed and then a tidal wave of emotion crashed against my body. I had glanced the only seven words I needed to see.

> "Your offer of acceptance is conditional upon…"

In that moment, it felt like all my hard work until that point had paid off. I'd made it. My life was never going to be the same again.

~~~

Okay, okay - a little melodramatic, I know. Allow me the artistic licence. The day you received your offer may have been more or less dramatic than my semi-fictional depiction but for all of us it's a memorable day and the start of a new chapter of our lives.

The following six years provided amazing experiences but also tough challenges. Medical school raised a lot of questions and I spent a lot of time searching for answers.

I saw people sacrificing so much for a career in medicine and asked if this has to be the case. I spent long, unproductive periods on the wards and asked if there was a better way. I memorised the brachial plexus then forgot it again.

I explored how we can maximise our impact as doctors and came across some uncomfortable truths and perspective-changing ideas. I spent countless hours on scientific research without gaining much before realising a better approach. I asked myself how to know whether medicine is the right career for me.

I was surprised to find that there was no central resource offering guidance on these sorts of 'bigger picture' questions. There are plenty of textbooks detailing academic content, from the workings of the endocrine system to mechanisms of drug action, and there are many guiding resources outside of the context of medicine. However, there are no medicine-specific books which combine a wider-scale, 'meta' approach with practical, down-to-earth advice.

As a result, I spent a lot of time during my degree collating ideas and information from disparate sources across different disciplines and asking how this collective wisdom can be applied to medicine. This was time-consuming but made my medical school experience more enjoyable, fruitful and fulfilling.

Earlier this year, my younger sister received an offer to study Medicine. I have a strong desire for her to have a fantastic time at medical school and set herself up for a successful and fulfilling career. As no source of medical wisdom, of the nature described above, existed, I decided to make one for her and for all other medical students. And thus, this book was born. I hope that it enhances your medical school experience and your medical career.

~~~

Chapter 1 contains my toughest medical school experience and outlines two techniques for finding the optimum balance between work and play.

Chapter 2 draws on interviews of top-performing Cambridge University students, cognitive science research and over five hundred hours of personal teaching experience to outline four fundamental principles for learning faster.

Chapter 3 shares four ways to make the most of time on the wards and explains how to use the techniques of world-class performers to hone the skills required for medicine.

Chapter 4 explores how a future doctor can maximise their positive impact, find a career path they love and master their niche. I outline an effective approach for undertaking high-level self-education in any area, related to medicine or otherwise.

Chapter 5 explains where most students go wrong with scientific research, the best approach to take and a method for generating great ideas.

Chapter 6 explores how to develop excellent written and oral communication and the benefits of doing so at medical school.

There are then four further short chapters giving suggestions for dealing with the stresses of medicine, considering whether medicine is right for you, techniques for memorisation and lessons from great doctors.

Chapter 1: Medicine from Fifty Thousand Feet: Perspective, Targets and Limits

Studying medicine can be fantastic. There's an endless amount of knowledge that can be obtained. Gradually ascending this mountain of information can be enjoyable and rewarding.

It can be a satisfying feeling to go from ignorance to relative expertise in certain topics. There are other incentives to work hard to obtain this knowledge too, such as admiration from your peers, praise from your parents and points for your CV.

However, there is a common pitfall that this can create: **Working too hard for the sake of it.**

You may have heard this before a million times, but let me use a personal example to demonstrate a point.

In my first year of medical school I was aiming high. At the end of the year, I was disappointed with my result so I resolved to do better the following year. I made a lot of sacrifices; I skipped social events, spent less time with my friends and spent many late nights in the library. Half-way through the year, we had a full 'mock' exam and the hard work paid off; I achieved a mark that, based on projections from previous mock and actual marks, predicted I'd finish in the top 10 of our 400-person cohort.

However, my approach wasn't sustainable; before the end of the year I became apathetic, burnt out and achieved a good but, compared to my personal target, disappointing result once again.

The following summer I spend a lot of time reflecting. My approach that year contributed to me breaking up with my girlfriend, feeling more distant from my friends and family and ultimately feeling less happy. I had sacrificed so much – what had it all been for?

I began to assess my motives. For a long time, I had been telling myself "I need to study hard so that I can be the best doctor I can be" but I realised this didn't hold up to scrutiny: the difference between a good and a great result wouldn't make me a much better doctor, yet the reduced life experiences from living in the library may well make me a worse one.

I realised that being the best had become part of my identity during school, causing me to lose perspective on how important it really is relative to other areas of life. I also realised that I cared too much about what other people thought of me and part of my motivation was to prove myself to others and show everyone how smart I was.

I want to stress that I don't think that working extremely hard is a bad thing. On the contrary, I think it is important and admirable to work hard towards a worthy goal. Most people don't work hard enough. However, we must be clear about our priorities, honest about our motives and strive to maintain perspective at all times.

I appreciate it is not that simple. If I had told my second-year self that exams aren't the be-all and end-all, I doubt he would have listened. I needed that tough summer of soul-searching to figure things out. Sometimes you just have to make your own mistakes and learn from your own experiences.

Assessing your priorities and maintaining perspective can be a continuous journey, one that is facilitated by reflection. A lot of us reflect informally, but there can be additional benefit from certain methods of formal, structured reflection. Two such techniques are 'Following the Trail of Whys' and 'Attending Your Own Funeral'.

Follow the Trail of Whys

It is easy to ask 'why' and accept the response, even when it doesn't really answer the question. For example:

Q: Why was the patient's intravenous fluid run at the wrong rate?

A: Because the previous nurse didn't change the run rate.

If we accept this answer without probing further, we will assume that this was the nurse's fault and that she should be blamed or held accountable in some way. However, this doesn't get to the bottom of the problem and is not a solution.

The founder of Toyota, Sakichi Toyoda, is credited with advising people to "Ask why five times." The exact number is not important, but continually asking why can be effective at finding new answers and uncovering flaws in previous assumptions.

Let me demonstrate with the above example:

1. **Why was the patient's intravenous fluid run at the wrong rate?**

The previous nurse didn't change the run rate.

2. **Why didn't the previous nurse change the rate?**

The doctor's order had gone to the pharmacy and the medication administration record (MAR) was not updated.

3. **Why wasn't the MAR updated?**

The MAR is updated only once per day.

4. **Why is the MAR updated only once per day?**

The hospital has chosen to use oral instructions for updates that happen more frequently.

5. **Why are oral instructions used?**

The process was constructed a decade ago, when medication orders changed less frequently due to longer lengths of stay. Upon further study, the hospital determines that 40 to 50 percent of its medications change every day.

It isn't until the fifth *why* that the <u>actual</u> answer to the question is found.

This technique can be applied to any situation, including understanding why you think or act in a certain way.

If I had been honest and objective with myself during my first two years of university, the Trail of Whys may have produced something like this:

1. **Why do you study so hard?**

Because I want to get one of the highest marks.

2. **Why do you want to get one of the highest marks?**

Because I want to show everyone that I'm the best.

3. **Why do you want to show everyone that you're the best?**

Because I derive some of my sense of self-worth from what others think of me.

4. **Why do you derive your sense of self-worth from what others think of you?**

Because my upbringing taught me to seek the approval of others. This was an adaptive response to my environment but is not serving me well while studying a competitive course at a competitive university.

Therefore, the solution is to deliberately re-appraise how I evaluate myself, rather than to focus on how hard I am studying or working.

Self-honesty and objectivity is important in really getting to the bottom of things when using this technique.

It's a very simple concept which can be applied very broadly; to understand an academic concept, to understand how a system works or, as above, to understand yourself.

Attend your own funeral

This technique involves visualising your own funeral, imagining how it could go and how you want it to go. The aim is that, by doing so, you will appreciate what really matters and is most important to you. There is a wider philosophy termed 'memento mori', meaning 'remember that you have to die', which believes meditating on our death can bring profound insights about ourselves.

A palliative care nurse called Bronnie Ware revealed the five most common regrets that people have at the end of their lives:

1. I wish I'd had the courage to live a life true to myself, not the life others expected of me.
2. I wish I hadn't worked so hard.
3. I wish I'd had the courage to express my feelings.
4. I wish I had stayed in touch with my friends.
5. I wish that I had let myself be happier.

Below is a description of the technique, from the book 'The Charisma Myth' by Olivia Fox Cabane. It can stir up emotions, so you are encouraged to do it in an environment where you feel comfortable being emotional and with time to process things after the exercise.

Set the scene and involve your senses:
- *Sit or lie down, close your eyes, and set the scene.*

- *Where is your funeral being held? What day of the week? What time of day? What is the weather like?*

- *See the building where the ceremony is being held. See people arriving. Who's coming? What are they wearing?*

- *Now move into the building and look around inside. Do you see flowers? If so, smell the flowers' scent heavy on the air.*

- *See people coming through the door. What are they thinking?*

- *What kind of chairs are they sitting in? What do these chairs feel like?*

Watch your funeral:

- *Think of the people you care most about or whose opinions matter most to you. What are they thinking?*

- *See them stepping up one after another and delivering their eulogy. What are they saying? What regrets do they have for you?*

- *Now think: What would you like them to have said? What regrets do you have for yourself?*

- *See people following your coffin to the cemetery and gathering around your grave. What would you like to see written on your tombstone?*

For a recording of the above guided exercise, visit http://foxcabane.com/audio/Funeral.mp3.

Other techniques

List the different elements of your life (spending time with your family, studying to achieve exam success, going to parties, etc.) and then give relative scores for how important each one is to you (such as a mark out of 10). Consider how much time you actually spend doing each activity and ask whether you would like to change this.

Ask what your motives are for the things that you do. Be honest with yourself. It's fine to have 'less honourable' motives such as 'money', 'respect' or 'the look on other people's faces when I answer a difficult question in a lecture', but being aware of them is useful.

Talk to a friend about what they think is important. Reflect on the similarities and differences in your priorities and the reasons for them.

A Canadian psychologist called Jordan Peterson founded the "Self Authoring" suite which encourages people to use writing to understand past events and plan for your ideal future. One exercise is as follows:

Think about your life in the future. Imagine that everything has gone as well as it possibly could. You have worked hard and succeeded at accomplishing all of your life goals. Think of this as the realization of all of your life dreams. Now, write about what you have imagined.

A friend of mine from medical school wrote a great article about how he approaches exams by viewing them as a game: http://bit.do/exams-game.

Set limits, not just targets

Learning medicine can consume your life. With clearer understanding of your priorities, you can set not only more appropriate targets but you can also set limits.

It may be that you still want to aim to finish top in your medical school, and that's fine. However, you may be content with a more modest target. For example, after my summer of reflection I set my target as finishing in the top 25% of all exams alongside enjoying life, spending time with friends and family and investing time and energy into other pursuits.

This limited the amount of time I spent studying and gave me more stress- and guilt-free time to enjoy. It also helped guide my studying. Whenever I came across new content, I would ask myself "would someone in the top 25% know this?" In some cases, the answer was "definitely yes", in which case I would work hard to learn it as efficiently as possible, using techniques I shall outline in Chapter 2. In other cases, the answer was "probably not", in which case I <u>decidedly did not learn it</u>. As well as saving time, I found my studying was more consistent, as were my results.

Don't get me wrong, I still work hard. But now I vent that same energy and determination into goals that I consider more worthwhile and more in-line with my deeper intrinsic values. I will elaborate upon this in Chapter 4.

One fear that some medical students have is that if they don't study as much as they can, they won't pass their exams. However, if you are intelligent enough to get into medical school then you are definitely smart enough to pass exams with the right approach. If you feel like this, you will benefit a lot from the principles of learning that I outline in Chapter 2. By taking the approach I outline in this book, I spent less time studying yet achieved better results.

~~~

CHAPTER 1 SUMMARY

- Studying medicine is competitive, there is an endless amount to learn and there are continuous exams. This means that many people sacrifice too much for work.
- Perspective and clarity can be increased by following the 'Trail of Whys' and 'attending your own funeral'.
- This enables us to set targets and limits. Limits can increase studying efficiency and help us find a good work-life balance.

Chapter 2: The Fundamentals of Fast Learning

Let me tell you about Balraj.

He was a student in my year at university who absolutely loved medicine. He went to all the lectures and spent many late nights in the library studying. In his free time, he'd read research articles, attend conferences and keep up-to-date with the medical world.

The problem was: he was struggling.

Each year, the course would build on content from previous years. He found it increasingly difficult to remember content that had already been covered and so found it harder and harder to keep up with new material. This came to a head in our fourth year, when he failed the exams and had to re-sit them.

Afterwards, we sat down together and tried to understand why. He was a smart student and had aced his exams throughout school. Why was he working harder than everyone else but still failing?

Many medical students will sympathise with this feeling of working endlessly but always feeling behind.

Medicine is tough. We're expected to learn huge amounts of content and are continually tested on it throughout medical school and our career. "Medicine is a career of life-long learning", we're told.

Throughout medical school, I saw the different approaches that my friends and colleagues took and the results they achieved. I was given the opportunity to spend over five hundred hours teaching students, including Cambridge medical undergraduates. I saw what worked well and what didn't.

One thing that I learnt is that it's not the raw level of intelligence that determines success at medical school. It's also not just how hard you work. I saw smart people do poorly and less smart people do exceptionally well. Rather, the most important thing is <u>how</u> you work.

At school we're taught many things but we're never really taught <u>how</u> to study. Yet there is a lot of research looking at the principles of memory formation and effective learning. Different people learn in different ways but many people go their whole lives without fully understanding how to maximise their personal capabilities.

The benefits of 'learning how to learn' can yield rewards for the rest of our medical careers, enabling us to perform better and to have more free time for other things.

From my students, friends and personal research, I found that the four most important principles of efficient learning are Spaced Repetition, learning for understanding, creating the conditions for deep work and facilitating continual improvement.

Spaced Repetition

Spaced repetition involves reviewing content at gradually increasing intervals. Research has shown that it dramatically increases the memory retention and thus efficiency of learning[1]. The first scientist to demonstrate this phenomenon was Ebbinghaus[2].

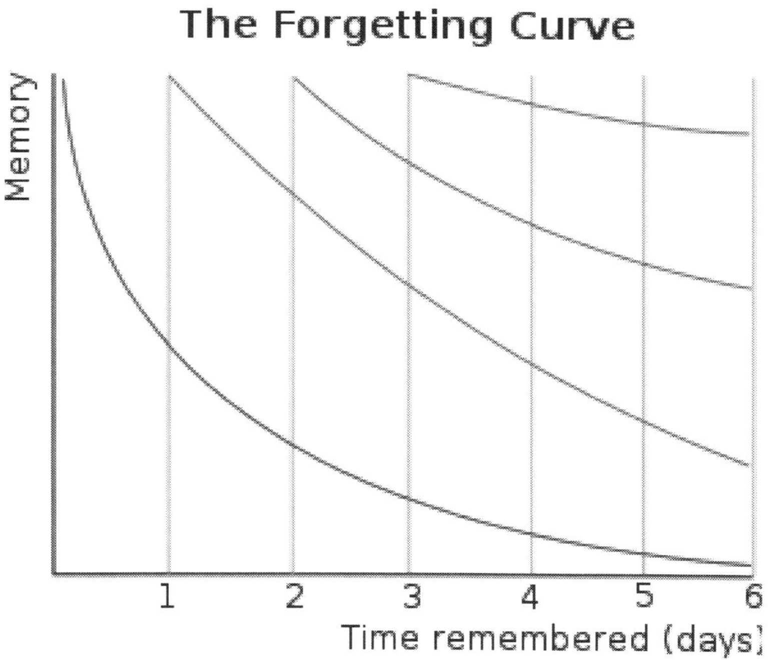

Fig 1. Ebbinghaus forgetting curve

A practical way to use this in medicine is as follows: when you learn some new information, recall it from memory and review

---

[1] Melton, "The Situation with Respect to the Spacing of Repetitions and Memory."
[2] "Classics in the History of Psychology -- Ebbinghaus (1885/1913) Chapter 1."

your notes after about one hour, then one day, then one week, then one month, then six months and then one year.

The principle is more important than the exact time spacing and can be adjusted around your life and schedule as required. You can organise this in a number of ways, on the micro (facts and concepts) and macro (topics) levels.

Micro (facts) level

One option for the micro level is to use electronic aids, such as Anki (where you can make your own flashcards) and Memrise (where you can use those created by others). These present you with flashcards and will re-present them at increasing intervals, based on your ease of recollection.

I found Anki most useful for fuelling active recall by having a condition name or an important concept on one 'side' of the card and lots of reference information copied from my notes on the back.

For example, Anki presents the card like this:

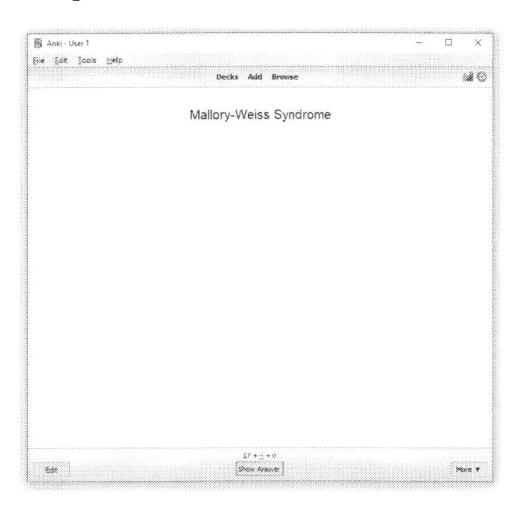

I would then spend about thirty seconds writing out as much as I can about Mallory-Weiss Syndrome (often using the rough format; aetiology, signs and symptoms, pathophysiology, complications, investigations, treatment).

I would then click 'show answer' at which point it would show the reference information, as below, for me to see how much I got and what I missed out.

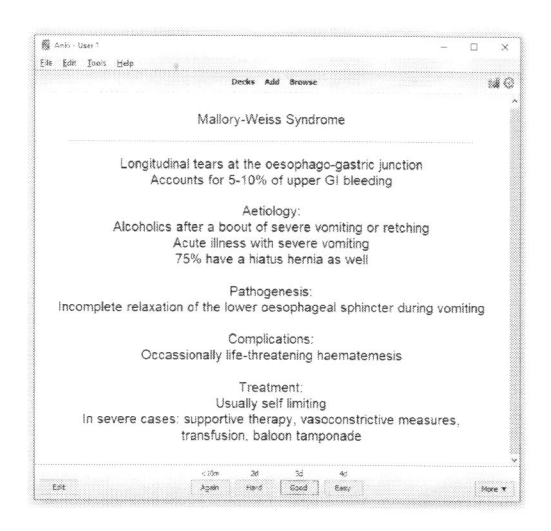

Based on how easy I found it and how much I was able to recall, I would select the appropriate option at the bottom and would then be re-presented with this card after the relevant period of time.

Macro (topics) level

I created a Review System which is easily organised through a central document as shown below. This is only one way to incorporate Spaced Repetition, but I will explain it to demonstrate the principle.

REVIEW SYSTEM

PRIORITY ORDER
1. NOT EMAILS
2. (any urgent work with imminent deadlines)
3. TODAY: anything to enter the Review System
4. REVIEWS: DAILY, WEEKLY, MONTHLY, SIX MONTHLY (in that order)
5. 'TO DO' TASKS
6. OTHER RELEVANT STUDY (eg. Upcoming topics or tests)
7. 'CATCH UP' STUDY (any notes that missed out from Review System)

To do
- Create central antibiotics document
- Schema for neck lumps

Daily reviews
- Dermatology blistering skin disease clinic
- Dr Samson teaching session 1

Weekly reviews

w/c Jan 23rd
- Dermatology intro lecture
- Infectious hepatology leture
- Diabetes and endocrinology tutorial
- Mixed teaching 19th Jan
- Testicular pathology
- Haematology interpretation algorithms

w/c Jan 30th

Monthly reviews

Jan
- Cardiology review
- Major Adult Diseases placement review

Feb

Six-monthly reviews

Feb/March
- Obstetrics and Gynaecology - full rev

March/April
Full reviews of:
- Neurology
- Rheumatology
- Orthopaedics

The system works as follows:

At the end of each day, I spend about an hour recapping things that I have seen, learnt and been taught that day. Anything worth reviewing the next day is added to the 'Daily Reviews' column.

At some point during the following day, I will review topics in the 'Daily Reviews' column (by recalling content from memory and often doing some further study to clarify important concepts). If I feel the topic is worth reviewing again, I will move the topic into the 'Weekly Reviews' column. This means that I will review it again in approximately one week's time and perform the same process (putting some into the 'Monthly Reviews' column and so on). Some smaller topics will be grouped into larger topics as they progress right-wards.

Here's how this works on a daily basis:

Whenever I have a free moment during the day (such as between teaching sessions, before a clinic, between theatre operations or any other time when no learning opportunities are present), I open up the central document and work through the topics for review in the priority order shown above, from left to right. This usually involves grabbing a piece of paper and recalling as much as I can on the topic before later referring to my notes (which I sync to my phone). If necessary, the recall can be purely mental, such as if bored during a long operation.

I have found using this system a very effective way to make the most of gaps during the day. I can recount numerous occasions where I had a gap of 10-30 minutes, during which previously I would have killed time checking my phone or emails, but instead reviewed some content. I would often get home in the evening having covered the majority of my reviews during the day so I had the option of taking the evening off knowing I'd made good progress.

I would estimate that this system alone enabled me to spend 30-40% less time studying with a noticeable improvement in long-term retention. It also meant I was far less stressed during exam period, particularly finals, as the majority of the content was in my long-term memory thus reducing the need to 'cram'.

Learn for understanding

People fall on a spectrum from those who predominantly learn for memorisation to those who predominantly learn for understanding[3]. Learning for understanding leads to higher percentage retention and for longer periods of time. Abstract facts

---

[3] Mayer, *Rote Versus Meaningful Learning.*

leak out of your brain, whereas *understanding* provides the context that will enable longer retention.

Tim Urban explains an analogy that compares knowledge of a topic to a tree[4]:

> *"If you don't fully get it, it's like a tree in your head with no trunk—and without a trunk, when you learn something new about the topic—a new branch or leaf of the tree—there's nothing for it to hang onto, so it just falls away. By [developing understanding], I build a tree trunk in my head, and from then on, all new information can hold on, which makes that topic forever more interesting and productive to learn about."*

I remember in my first year, I memorised the mechanisms the kidneys use to help maintain homeostasis. While I did well in my physiology exam, I couldn't even remember the mechanisms by the end of the summer. When I started meeting patients with renal disease on the ward a few years later I realised how this approach missed the point. Learning the content is not just so you can pass the exams. I re-learnt the renal physiology but this time made sure I understood the bigger picture and the clinical relevance. As a result, I can still remember it today and continue to apply the knowledge in clinical situations.

In medicine, it can feel like we don't have time to develop a real understanding of a topic because there is so much to learn. We are often assessed in ways that directly test our factual recollection rather than our understanding, such as multiple-choice or true/false questions. As a result, it can be easy to focus on rote

---

[4] Urban, *The Elon Musk Blog Series*.

learning as many facts as possible. While it requires slightly more initial effort to develop the base understanding, the greater retention makes it much more efficient in the long-run. It also better serves the real aim of medical school which is to become good doctors rather than to pass exams.

It's not always clear to ourselves where we fall on the spectrum of memorisation vs understanding. It can be easy to assume we understand something well, only for this mirage to fade when something highlights the gaps. However, increasing the amount that we learn by understanding is a habit that can be trained. Again, this can be done on micro (concepts) and macro (topics) levels.

For a more in-depth analysis of the levels of understanding, visit:
http://lesswrong.com/lw/1yq/understanding_your_understanding/

Micro (concepts) level

The **Feynman method** is a useful way to identify any gaps in understanding of a concept and how to solve them:

1. **Select a concept.**
2. **See if you can explain it in a way that a 5-year-old would understand.**
    - If you can, rest assured that you understand it.
    - If not, there is one of three areas that you may need to address: understanding, memory and simplicity. Based on the area, consider the following questions:

3. **Is there something you don't understand?** -> actively search for the information and understanding to fill this gap.

4. **Are you having difficulty remembering certain parts?** -> think of an analogy you can use which will make it easier to remember

5. **Are you confident you understand and remember it but are having difficulty explaining it?** -> think of a way to simplify the concept. Is there anything you can remove while still making sense?

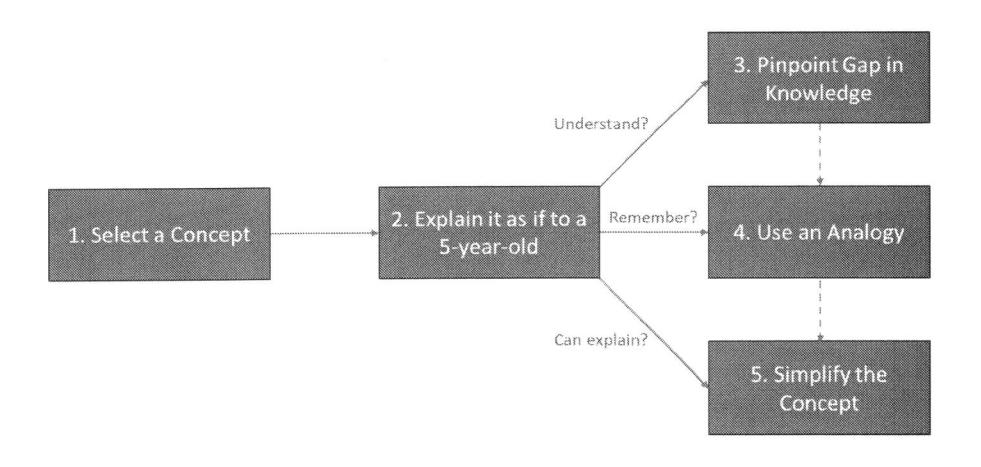

```
1. Select a Concept --> 2. Explain it as if to a 5-year-old
    Understand? --> 3. Pinpoint Gap in Knowledge
    Remember? --> 4. Use an Analogy
    Can explain? --> 5. Simplify the Concept
```

I shall demonstrate this method using the example of how the kidney regulates blood pressure.

1. *Select a concept.*

How the kidney regulates blood pressure. So far, so good.

2. **See if you can explain it in a way that a 5-year-old would understand.**

The explanation to a five-year-old would be something along the lines of: *"Our body stores lots of water. In the water, there is a lot of salt (like the salt you put on your fish and chips). Wherever the salt goes, the water follows. High blood pressure means you have too much water in your body. When this happens, the kidney gets rid of salt and water follows it. This goes into your bladder and later you wee it out. When the blood pressure is low, what does this mean? (you have too little water in your body) So what do you think the kidney does? (holds onto more salt so less water is peed out)"*

Note: It may not always be necessary to appeal to a five-year-old's toilet humour... but it can help.

3. **Is there something you don't understand?**

Let's say this explanation makes you realise you don't understand *how* the kidney gets rid of salt. You would then consult notes on the mechanisms used. Even if you do not remember all of the specific mechanisms, having learnt deeper will make it more likely that you remember the key surface concept.

4. **Are you having difficulty remembering certain parts?**

If you are not sure you will remember the concept, then you can think of an analogy. This can be quite abstract as long as it holds true as the main purpose is to help you remember things. For example, let's use ketchup to remember how the kidney regulates blood pressure: When pressure is high (i.e. you squeeze hard on the ketchup bottle), lots of salty ketchup comes out, whereas when pressure is low (you squeeze softly) then much less does. (You could expand the analogy by saying that when the lid is on it causes hydronephrosis but let's not over-complicate things here...)

5. *Are you confident you understand and remember it but are having difficulty explaining it?*

Let's say we over-complicated our explanation by talking about 'blood pressure' which a five-year-old may not understand. This is something that we could simplify to talking about the amount of water in the body.

Think of a concept now and practise this method.

If you can't think of one, here are some suggestions (in increasing difficulty):

- How muscles move body parts
- Antibiotic resistance
- The Theory of Evolution

~~~

Albert Einstein reportedly once said:

'If you can't explain it to a six-year-old, you don't understand it yourself'.

~~~

Another technique that facilitates learning for understanding is **"Following the Trail of Whys"**, as explored in Chapter 1.

Macro (topics) level

Before you learn or review a topic, assess your current state of understanding by asking yourself the following questions:

- **What do you already know about the topic?** (Write out as much as you can from memory)

- **What don't you know? What don't you understand?**

The purpose of asking these questions is to highlight gaps in your knowledge or memory which you can then fill. Use them to write a set of questions to have in the back of your mind as you study, to act as a mental prompt and keep you on track. When you're finished, check that you can now answer these questions from memory.

Afterwards, to check whether you do truly understand the content you must actively test yourself. Useful ways to do so include:

- **Recall the information from memory.** For example, write a three-sentence summary of what you have learnt, write a short essay or make a poster or integrative diagram — you can be creative.

- **Practise exam questions** (if learning for an exam) — don't wait until someone else sets them for you or for the exam itself; find your own and see which you can answer and which you can't!

Create conditions for deep work

Some argue that the ability to maintain deep focus is one of the most valuable skills in the modern day, but that in an age of distractions, internet and high-paced life, it is becomingly increasingly rare[5].

By fostering our ability to maintain focus, we can reach greater depths of understanding. When probing something intellectually, understanding is obtained gradually. Each answer raises another question to be answered. Becoming distracted disrupts this, inhibiting the depth of understanding you can reach.

The ability to concentrate deeply enables you to achieve in one study session more than you may otherwise achieve in multiple, fragmented sessions. It is not as simple as just covering more content. If you cover something properly and really understand it, you won't need to re-learn it in the same way again. This links back to the idea of learning for understanding.

Deep focus can also save time by helping you to think more clearly in real-time about the approach you are taking. You may realise that what you are doing isn't working and think of a better way. This can be further reinforced by a formal Weekly Review which I will discuss later.

Csikszentmihalyi is a psychologist who described the concept of 'Flow', where we are completely immersed in a task and the sense of time and space disappears. It relies on an optimal matching of the difficulty of the task with our abilities; challenging but not overwhelmingly so.

---

[5] Newport, "Deep Work: Rules for Focused Success in a Distracted World."

The ability to sustain focus and enter 'flow' when required may not always come naturally. But over time, we can train our ability to do so. This ability stretches our cognitive capacities and increases our abilities to solve difficult problems in the real world.

To foster this ability, we must remove distractions, use social media on our own terms and actively train ourselves to focus for set periods. I shall explore these in turn.

Remove distractions

This may sound obvious, but distractions can be a huge hindrance to productivity. Five minutes spent checking emails or Facebook leads to far more than five minutes of time wasted as it takes time and effort for your mind to regain focus on the original task. Often, allowing yourself to be distracted is the easy way out of a doing a difficult task.

Our brains are hard-wired to detect and respond to novel stimuli so avoiding distractions can be difficult, regardless of our willpower. Therefore, to make it easier for ourselves we must set up as many barriers as possible for distractions.

If you are often distracted by your phone, turn it off or put it in another room. If there's a website you spend a lot of time on, block it. If there's something or someone that distracts you, find somewhere to study where that won't be a problem. Don't make excuses to yourself — work around whatever obstacles may arise.

My personal biggest source of distraction is the internet. I find it so easy to get lost in the recesses of the internet and lose track of time. I realised that I needed to solve this problem in order to get anything done. I came across the following apps, without which I would never have finished this book:

- **InternetOff app** – lets you have the internet switched off as default, and need a password to switch the internet on for a period of time.

- **'StayFocusd' extension for Chrome** – lets you limit time spent on certain websites or block them entirely.

By removing distractions, we can complete our work quicker and therefore find more time to do things that we really enjoy.

Use social media on your own terms

Social media can be a massive time-sink. I often found I'd log into Facebook "for a 5-minute break" or to check something only to find myself scrolling down the Newsfeed an hour or two later. The following are things that I set up to reduce the frequency with which I log on to Facebook and the amount of time spent when I do:

- I **changed my password** into a series of letters, numbers and symbols and wrote it down on a bit of paper. I put this in a drawer along with a few relevant inspirational quotes and other stimuli that will make me think twice before deciding to log in.

- I downloaded the **'News Feed Eradicator for Facebook'** Google Chrome extension, which replaces your newsfeed with an inspirational quote.

In my opinion, the three main benefits of Facebook are event invitations, messaging friends and sharing things with others. Therefore, I set up ways to do them without needing to log in to Facebook:

- I changed my settings so that I receive **email notifications for event invitations**. When I get an email, I write the event in my calendar. As long as I know about the event, I can talk to my other friends who are attending and will be aware of any changes in date or time plus other relevant details.

- I **downloaded the Facebook Messenger app without the main Facebook app** so that I can still message friends without needing to log on to the central Facebook.

- I use other apps to share things on Facebook – **Instagram** for photos and **Buffer** for sharing posts (Buffer has the added benefit of letting you decide when you want your posts to be shared).

These enabled me to get the main benefits of Facebook without wasting too much time. If you feel you spend more time on social media than you would like, consider trying some of the above techniques or coming up with your own.

There are other side effects of social media not directly related to productivity which can be insidious. It can increase how much you care about what others think and it can cause you to compare yourself more with others. This may explain why some recent studies show that social media can have a negative effect on satisfaction.

If you often consider your approach to social media, Cal Newport (an American computer science professor and author[6]) makes a case for not using it altogether in a TED talk (https://www.youtube.com/watch?v=3E7hkPZ-HTk) and I have

---

[6] "Follow a Sunday Ritual - Study Hacks - Cal Newport."

written an article about my experiences and current approach at chrislovejoy.co.uk/facebook.

The Pomodoro Method

One simple technique that can have a dramatic effect on study efficiency is the Pomodoro method. In short, it involves alternating 25 minutes of undisrupted work with 5-minute breaks. For a fuller explanation see this video by Thomas Frank: https://www.youtube.com/watch?v=H0k0TQfZGSc.

Some points that maximise the benefit from it include:

- Having a fixed timer which does it for you (rather than setting and re-setting alarms) is helpful: for example, the physical Pomodoro timer, tomato-timer.com for in-browser or Tomighty as a desktop app.

- Sticking diligently to the timings (of 25-5-25-5), so you can plan exactly how many 'pomodoros' you will do before lunchtime, say, or another commitment.

- Doing something that you enjoy or doing exercise during the 5-minute breaks (away from the computer/study area). I will do small admin stuff if I have a lot (for example, washing dishes, doing laundry), otherwise I will skim a book chapter, read a short blog post or listen to a favourite song. Doing short bursts of exercise, such as squats, planks or sit-ups, can both bring your energy level up and be a good way to squeeze in exercise to free up time later. I often find the first one or two pomodoros of a day quite difficult but am re-energised by later ones.

- Alternating it with some other approach – I personally found morning Pomodoros followed by less-structured afternoon study sessions more effective.

Meditation is similar in that for a period of time you continually bringing your attention back to an object of focus. There is an increasing body of evidence to support that it can improve concentration. Popular apps such as Headspace and Calm can help with this.

~~~

In Deep Work, Cal Newport advises us:

"Don't Take Breaks from Distraction. Instead Take Breaks from Focus."

~~~

Facilitate continual improvement

The techniques I've outlined above are some of the fundamentals of efficient learning. However, different people will gain different amounts from each point. Learning to learn faster is an individualised process and is not as simple as just following a list of steps or using some techniques that someone tells you.

This brings me on to the fourth fundamental principle which is to **facilitate continual improvement.** This involves continuous experimentation and evaluation. Useful ways to increase the rate of improvement are to obtain feedback and act upon it, reflect weekly and always look for new ideas.

Feedback

Feedback is a fundamental requirement for improvement. It enables us to continually correct our course. Imagine driving on a road with no road markings, or throwing darts at a dart board while blind-folded.

Give yourself feedback by asking the following questions after each event:

1. What worked well?
2. Where could you improve?

Ask other people for feedback. Be accepting of this feedback! If someone is giving you criticism or something you don't agree with, don't step in and defend yourself — keep silent for as long as you can and then reflect on what they have told you. Aim to view yourself as objectively as possible.

Use objective assessment methods. For example, do past questions in timed conditions and then mark them. If essays are part of your assessment, write some and ask someone else to mark them. This objectivity forces you to be aware of your current stage and avoids unwarranted optimism.

Weekly Review

Cal Newport has written about how a Weekly Review can increase short-term productivity and lead to long-term improvement. It involves setting aside some time each week (I usually spend an hour or two on Saturday morning) to assess how the previous week went, what you can try in the upcoming week and structuring your week.

Short-term productivity is increased by deciding a structure in advance. It makes you more likely to complete a task on a particular day. If you have a series of different tasks lined up for subsequent days, you are more likely to ensure that you find time to do them and less likely to postpone them if you 'don't feel like it'.

In the long-term, Weekly Reviews facilitate improvement through continual self-assessment. You may realise certain inefficiencies in your approach and think of ways to solve them. These solutions may in themselves lead to new problems. Continually looking for ways to improve can lead to dramatic improvements in the long-term.

A Weekly Review can be used in contexts outside of academic pursuits. Benjamin Franklin reportedly chose a virtue to work on each week and at the end of the week reviewed how well he had kept to it.

For the Weekly Review, you can ask yourself the following questions.

Assess performance that week

- Did I get everything done that I wanted to? (If not, why not?)
- What aspects of my approach worked well?
- What areas could be improved?

Planning the upcoming week

- What do I want to achieve? What material do I want to cover?

- When will I achieve it?

- What new approaches/techniques can I try this week?

Always look for new ideas

There is an inexhaustible amount of information available on learning theory, study tips and techniques. Your aim is to find those that work best for you; cherry-pick from the information available and if they work, use them – if they don't, discard them.

For example, a friend of mine, who came top in the year on more than one occasion, has written an entertaining guide on memorisation. It explores four techniques; mnemonics, method of loci and story associations, the Major System technique and synesthetic memory. It is very useful for the times when there is little space for 'understanding' and you just have to memorise the facts. For more details, see the chapter "Memorisation Techniques". Try the techniques he describes and see if they work for you.

There are a many sources of study advice on the internet. Ones I have found useful include:

- **Thomas Frank**, who founded **CollegeInfoGeek** and posts videos on his Youtube Channel: https://www.youtube.com/user/electrickeye91

- **Cal Newport**, a computer science professor who runs the **"Study Hacks blog"**: http://calnewport.com/blog/

CHAPTER 2 SUMMARY

- Learning faster improves your academic results and gives you more time to do other things.
- Spaced Repetition and learning for understanding enhance long-term retention.
- Flash cards and a Review System can enforce Spaced Repetition.
- The Feynman Method, question-based learning and active recall can increase understanding.
- Developing the ability to focus is an invaluable skill today. To develop it, we should remove distractions, consider our relationship with social media and try the Pomodoro Method.
- Learning is individualised and life-long. Continual improvement can be facilitated by obtaining feedback, objective self-assessments weekly and always searching for new ideas.

Chapter 3: Mastering Clinical Medicine

"What do you think is wrong?", the consultant asked.

I had no idea.

I looked back at the patient that I had just examined, lying on the bed in front of me, hoping for a clue.

"Err… a problem with his bowels… awaiting surgery?", I answered.

A flash of disappointment crossed the consultant's face.

He grabbed my hand, took it over to the patient and used it to prod the patient in the right upper quadrant.

"Do you feel that? That's his liver. It's 3-4 cm below the costal margin. He has hepatomegaly (an enlarged liver)."

We left the patient's bed side and wrapped up the teaching session.

The frustrating thing was I had actually felt that liver during my original examination, I just hadn't realised that it was large.

I'd performed abdominal examinations stacks of times before. My routine was slick. I knew the appropriate technique for palpating the liver. I'd been taught how you should bend from the metacarpophalangeal joint and to always keep your hand in contact with the abdomen.

I could also reel off causes of hepatomegaly, from alcoholic liver disease to infectious hepatitis, from malignancy to heart failure. (Of course, I'd learnt this well using Spaced Repetition and learning for understanding!)

Despite all of this, in that moment I missed the diagnosis. For all my slickness and knowledge, I hadn't achieved the fundamental purpose of the examination.

It wasn't that I hadn't been spending time on the wards. I had been coming in every day, joining the ward round in the morning and helping with jobs in the afternoon.

The problem was: this isn't a how you learn to recognise hepatomegaly.

~~~

The techniques described in Chapter 2 are great for the sit-down-and-study type of learning. Thankfully, not all of medicine is like that. We must also learn a whole host of ward-based skills, from taking blood to examining patients to working in a team. We must learn to appreciate the variation between individuals; how the same condition may present differently in two different people or how one patient wants all the details, and another only wants the key points. We must learn, for example, what is a normal-sized liver and what is hepatomegaly.

These are skills that can't be learnt from a textbook. It won't teach us to appreciate natural variation or how to respond to new situations. For this, we must spend time on the ward.

Yet it's also possible to spend a lot of time on the wards without developing these skills much either. Some approaches are more effective than others. In this chapter I will explore how to make the most of time in clinical settings and how to deconstruct clinical skills in order to master them.

Making the most of clinical time

Unfortunately (for you), the clinical environment is designed to <u>treat patients</u> rather than to <u>train medical students</u>. This means it's up to you to take the initiative. It is very easy to spend time on the ward, thinking that you're a good student for being there, without learning very much at all.

To get the most out of your time, you should always have an objective, not be afraid to leave, tag onto good teachers and link your experiences to your reading.

<u>Always have an objective</u>

So much happens in a hospital on any given day. It's easy to just go with the flow and hope that you passively absorb all the things you need to. With this approach you may have the occasional great clinical experience and will gradually pick up the required knowledge and skills with enough time. However, the more self-directed you are, the quicker you can learn and the better you can become.

This is achieved by deciding your objective in advance. For me, this involved making a weekly priority list (during my weekly review, described in Chapter 2) as well as a daily objective list. At the end of each evening, I would take a piece of A4 paper and fold it in half three times. On this, I would write six things that I would like to achieve the following day, as in the example below. I would carry this in my pocket at all times, and cross things off when I achieved them, providing a small sense of achievement each time. Sometimes I would add a priority order by numbering them 1-6.

An example of my priority six:
- Write in patient notes
- Take blood from ≥3 patients
- Recognise hepatomegaly
- Understand Liver Function Tests (LFTs)
- See 2 or 3 endoscopies
- Understand 2 patient's cases from the ward in depth

This list can be tailored to the opportunities that you know you will have, for example if you know there is an endoscopy list tomorrow. When you write the objectives, you can think of ways you will achieve them. For example, for the list above you could plan to join the ward-round and ask to write in the patient notes (1) as well as choosing two interesting patients from the ward-round to study later (6). You could ask to leave the ward-round early to attend endoscopy (5), then after lunch come back to the ward and ask if there are any bloods to be taken (2), any patients to examine with signs (3) and if any of the doctors are free to explain LFTs (4). However, it's important to be flexible as you can't always predict how things will go. Maybe the doctors won't let you write in the notes on the ward-round, or they are all too busy to teach you about LFTs. In these cases, you must be adaptable and seek alternative ways to achieve your aims, for example finding a guide on LFTs on the internet and then looking through the blood results of patients with deranged LFTs. Or maybe there are no patients in the hospital with hepatomegaly, in which case you can think of another sign you want to learn to recognise. It is on these days where having the objectives is so important, as otherwise you may spend a lot of time waiting around and achieve very little.

A great little book with suggestions for objectives is "101 things to do with spare moments on the ward" by Dason Evans and Nakul Patel. The title is self-explanatory.

Don't be afraid to leave

That being said, there will be days where despite your objectives and your enthusiasm, there is just too little benefit to be gained from staying where you are. Perhaps the doctors are busy, you've seen all the patients with signs on examination and there's not much else to do. Don't feel an obligation to stay on the ward, in theatres or in clinics. Your time may be better spent elsewhere in the hospital or by going home and doing some study. If need be, excuse yourself with the phrase "I have teaching". Don't be afraid to attend multiple different theatres or clinics in the same morning or afternoon. It pays to have contingency plans in case a theatre case doesn't happen or a doctor in clinic isn't giving you any teaching.

Remember: you are not being paid and you are there for your own learning, so if you would learn more from leaving and doing something else then **do so**.

Tag on to good teachers

Sometimes you will have the good fortune of coming across a doctor who is (a) friendly, (b) keen to teach and (c) good at teaching. Tag on to them and milk them for all they are worth. Doctors who are good teachers can make a huge difference. As well as teaching you useful concepts, they can help direct your learning on the wards and get you involved with the team.

Newly qualified doctors ('F1s' in the UK) are often best as the content is still fresh in their minds and they may have more free time. However, a good registrar or consultant can provide greater depths of insight into their specialities.

If you want to be taught, make yourself teachable. Show enthusiasm and be proactive. Introduce yourself to the doctors. Ask questions when possible. Don't be put off if someone blows you off (it's not personal!).

One concern some students have is that they don't want to distract doctors or waste their time. However, when doctors teach medical students it is mutually beneficial. Explaining things to you will refresh their memory of important content. I really enjoy teaching so when an enthusiastic medical student is on my ward it makes things much more enjoyable.

In Chapter 6 I shall make the case for why you should also get some teaching experience while at medical school.

Link your experiences to your reading

It is often better to learn the academic and clinical components of medicine together, rather than in isolation.

Aim to spend at least an hour each evening doing follow-up reading based on what you saw that day. For example, if you saw an interesting patient with jaundice, read further about the different causes of jaundice and how you can distinguish them.

Our brain has been shown to remember stories far better than abstract facts. In medicine, these 'stories' can be the stories of individual patients that you meet. By meeting a patient with a particular condition, you create mental 'hooks' for you to hang academic information off, which will make it far easier to remember. For example, a friend of mine met a patient with Fournier's Gangrene in his fifth year and did some brief reading on it that evening. He never came across it again but during our final exams in sixth year, he remembered the patient he'd met and was able to answer a question on it. It is doubtful he would have remembered this had he either solely seen the patient or solely read about it in a textbook.

Linking patient experiences to reading can also be done on the ward by actively recalling your notes or previous knowledge when you see a patient with a particular condition. For example, if you meet a patient with Parkinson's disease, and you previously made notes about the condition and different treatment methods, actively recall as much from your memory as you can. I often carry a rough piece of paper in my pocket, which I will occasionally take out and scribble on as much as I can remember on a topic. It can be useful to later refer to your notes to fill in any gaps.

Deconstructing clinical skills

Any complex skill or activity can be broken down into parts. With more practice and experience, you become less conscious of the smaller parts and start to experience them as one whole integrated activity.

For example, when someone learns to play the piano they may start with one hand on the keyboard playing the five notes that rest under each finger. They may then learn to move their hand up and down to play notes of higher or lower pitches. Initially, they will learn both hands separately and later will play with both hands at the same time. In comparison, an experienced pianist playing a Beethoven sonata will not be consciously thinking about any of this. By that stage, the subcomponents of the skill have coalesced into one fluid process.

This is true also in medicine. When someone starts learning medicine, they must learn the key subcomponents, such as 'history-taking' (asking the patient questions about what's wrong) and the 'physical examination' (inspecting the patient's body for signs related to disease). These subcomponents can be further broken down; a history includes exploring the patient's main complaint, screening for other symptoms, exploring the patient's medical background, their social situation and other elements. An experienced doctor has the ability to integrate these skills and draw on the appropriate combinations as required.

When learning these skills, a useful approach is to deconstruct them into their smallest parts, analyse the best ways to learn each component and then re-integrate them. This is an approach that Tim Ferriss used to become world champion in Chinese kickboxing and set a World Record in Argentine tango. He even deconstructed how to make a good podcast, then used the principles to make a podcast asking world-class performers to deconstruct their performance. (Meta or what.)

I will use the example of mastering the 'physical examination' to demonstrate how I used these principles, although it can be applied to many aspects of learning medicine. While the specifics may be useful, I want to demonstrate the <u>process</u> which you can then apply in different ways and to different things.

I applied the same approach to history-taking, physical examination, practical skills such as taking bloods and cannulation, and interpreting investigations such as ECGs and X-rays. I also applied this principle outside of medicine. For example, I used it to go from being a beginner at basketball to representing my university within fifteen months and being awarded Most Valuable Player after another fifteen months.

Mastering the physical examination

At medical school, you must learn the 'formal' way to perform physical examinations which is rarely followed fully in clinical practice. Assessment is usually in an 'OSCE' format (Objective, Structured Clinical Examinations), which involves examining a patient's specific body system (for example, Cardiovascular, Respiratory, Neurological), then summarising the signs that you found and answering questions about it (the 'viva').

I divided OSCE-style physical examinations into four components:

- **The examination schema:** The specific sequence used and signs looked for. For the major systems (cardiovascular, respiratory and abdominal examinations), you usually start in the hands, work up the arms to the face, then down the body via the chest and abdomen to the legs).
- **Recognition of signs:** In every patient, the schema followed is the same but different patients will have different patterns of signs present. A skilled clinician recognises these signs in combination to point towards a

diagnosis, for example the combination of (i) nail clubbing, (ii) reduced chest expansion and (iii) fine crackles in the lungs is suggest of pulmonary fibrosis.
- **Presenting the findings:** After the examination, you must briefly summarise the signs (both positive signs and important negatives) and the possible diagnoses that they point towards.
- **Viva:** The examiner then asks follow-up questions about the possible conditions, distinguishing features and other information.

For each of these aspects of the examinations, I devised a plan for practising them until they became second nature.

The examination schema

As early as possible, create your own specific sequence for the examination. My advice is to look at multiple sources, decide on a logical structure and then create a central guide which you follow every time. You can make minor modifications based on feedback and teaching, but get as much practice as possible performing the same sequence in the same way until it becomes second nature.

Useful resources for creating your initial schema include websites such geekymedics.com and oscestop.co.uk or clinical examinations books such as Macleod's or Talley and O'Connor's.

In terms of the **structure**, it is useful to create 'hooks' that you can hang different parts of the examination off. For example, for the inspection part of the hand examination I have five hooks: (i) skin, (ii) nails, (iii) soft tissues, (iv) bones and (v) joints. Within each of these five there are a number of things to look for: e.g. when inspecting the (i) skin I'll look for rashes, nodules, scars, etc.; then, when looking at the (ii) nails I'll look for pitting, onycholysis, clubbing, etc. It is much easier to remember things in these domains than as a long separate list.

Think of as many useful ways for **remembering** different parts of the examination (rather than rote learning it all). For example, for the palpating and percussing part of the abdominal exam there are:

- <u>Two</u> things you palpate AND percuss (the liver and spleen)
- <u>Two</u> things you only palpate (the kidneys and the aorta)
- <u>Two</u> things you only percuss for (shifting dullness and bladder)
- <u>Two</u> things you auscultate (bowel sounds and bruits)

Once you have created the schema and thought of useful ways to remember it, the more practice, the better to make the examination as automatic as possible. As the old adage goes "One examination a day keeps finals at bay". Not having patients is no excuse; practise with your friends, on a teddy bear or even on your pillow!

Recognition of signs

The key to getting good at recognising patterns of signs is to see as many patients as possible on the wards and trying to figure out what is wrong with them – there is no real substitute. Initially, it is okay to know what condition the patient has before you see them so that you can see it and register "so *that's* what spider naevi look like". However, once you have a little experience you want to avoid as much as possible knowing what the patient's condition is before you meet them. This way you actively have to try and work out what they have and you will learn much more.

Another useful technique is to visualise the combination of signs you would expect to see in certain conditions. For example, choose a disease like Cushing's Disease or someone who had a renal transplant following renal failure – travel from head to toe imagining the signs you may see. When you run through practice examinations with your teddy bear/pillow/friends, choose a particular condition and imagine what signs you would pick up as you go along.

Presenting the findings

There is no 'right' way to present findings after an examination, although certain approaches are more effective than others. My advice is to experiment with different ways and find what works for you. The two most popular approaches are as follows.

1. **Following the rough order of the examination**

As an example, a patient with aortic stenosis:

"On examination of Mr Jones' cardiovascular system, I found him comfortable at rest with no evidence of oedema, cyanosis or anaemia and no peripheral stigmata of cardiovascular disease. His pulse is slow rising in character, the rate is 70 and regular and blood pressure is 120/95. The JVP is not raised. The apex beat is sustained and in the 5th inter-costal space. Heart sounds 1 and 2 were normal, with an added ejection systolic murmur hear loudest in the aortic region with radiation to the carotids.

*In conclusion, Mr Smith has a narrow pulse pressure, a sustained apex beat and an ESM which is in keeping with **aortic stenosis**."*

This is the easier method of the two. In advance, decide the 'hooks' you will use for each examination as it will make it much easier to remember. For example, using this method for the cardiovascular presentation, I would always have the opening sentence above, then mention pulse, JVP, apex beat and heart sounds in that precise order.

2. **Present only the main positive findings then important negative findings.**

For example, in a patient with aortic stenosis:

"On examination of Mr Jones' cardiovascular system, the main positive findings were a slow-rising pulse, narrow pulse pressure, displaced apex beat and ejection systolic murmur heard loudest in the aortic region with radiation to the carotids. This would be in keeping with aortic stenosis.

Notable negatives included no diastolic murmurs, no metallic heart sounds, no evidence of heart failure, including no peripheral oedema or crackles in the lungs, and no evidence of infective endocarditis, including no clubbing, Osler's nodes or Janeway lesions."

The notable negatives mentioned should be tailored to rule out other possible causes and possible consequences of the condition you concluded. For the above example, heart failure and infective endocarditis are both possible consequences of aortic stenosis.

This is a slightly more difficult method of presentation but if executed well can make you stand out.

My approach was to practise both methods and then select the one I was most comfortable with in the exam. If an examination went well and I was confident of the diagnosis, I would use the second method. If I was less confident, the first method was nice to fall back onto. A friend of mine, who did not want to have to decide during the exam, selected a preferred method and used it every time.

Again, practise as much as possible so that it becomes second nature. It can also be useful to practise presenting with different conditions in mind, to further reinforce your ability to recognise patterns of signs.

Viva

Common questions in the viva include "what is the differential diagnosis for X?" (for example, a systolic murmur, jaundice, hepatomegaly), "what investigations would you like to perform?" and "what would your management be?".

I prepared answers based on the most likely examination findings and the most common questions asked. For each, I thought of a logical structure for an answer and aimed for a top three or groups of three where possible. I created recordings where I would ask the question then leave a pause for me to answer before the recording gave the model answer that I prepared. I would listen to these recordings when I had free moments, such as when I was running errands in town or travelling somewhere, until they became second nature.

Below are two examples. If you would like access to the full set of recordings, contact me at: chris@medicalstudentmanual.com. I may upload them to my website in future so it's worth checking out http://chrislovejoy.co.uk.

1. What is the differential diagnosis for a systolic murmur?

- **Valvular problems**
    - AS / PS
    - MR / TR
- **Problems with the heart wall**
    - HOCM
    - ASD
    - VSD
- **Systemic conditions**
    - Hyperthyroidism
    - Anaemia
    - Pregnancy
    - Paget's disease of bone
- **Innocent murmur**

2. What investigations would you perform for some who has fainted?

To create this answer, I started by creating a list of the differential diagnosis (see below).

I then created an answer which covers the main differentials in the format (i) bedside tests, (ii) blood tests, (iii) imaging and (iv) special tests.

Differential diagnosis for a 'faint':

- **cardio**
    - vasovagal
    - postural hypertension (prolonged bedrest, drug induced, hypovolaemic, autonomic failure)
    - arrhythmias
    - MI
    - PE
- **neuro**
    - seizure
    - stroke
- **metabolic**
    - hypoglycaemia
    - alcohol
    - hypoxia
    - electrolyte abnormalities
    - uraemia
- **other**
    - hyperventilation
    - narcolepsy
    - pseudoseizures

Investigations:

- cardio and neuro exams
- bedside
    - lying and standing BP (for postural hypotension)
    - glucose (for hypoglycaemia)
    - ECG (for arrhythmias, MI, PE)
- bloods

- - FBC (for anaemia)
  - U+Es (for electrolyte abnormalities)
  - alcohol markers
- imaging
  - CT head/MRI (for stroke)
- special tests
  - EEG (for seizures)

Integration

As well as practising separate components, it is important to continually practise integrating them together. This can be done by finding a colleague and practising on each other or on patients, each time following the full schema, presenting findings and giving each other a viva. Examinations in pairs or threes are always best; you can take it in turns to examine and give each other feedback. It can be useful to keep a list of patients with signs which you can also share with colleagues.

~~~

CHAPTER 3 SUMMARY

- Hospitals are designed for treating patients and not training students so it is important to be proactive and confident.
- Make the most of your time by having an objective, not being afraid to leave, tagging on to good teachers and linking your experiences to reading.
- Doctors must learn separate skills, such as history-taking, examinations, practical skills and interpreting

investigations, and combine them in order to look after patients.
- These skills can be learnt effectively by deconstructing them into subcomponents, mastering them individually and practising their integration

Chapter 4: Make your Mark on the Medical Field (and the Power of Self-Education)

"... And that's why my friend quit medicine and became a banker."

It wasn't the conclusion I expected from a talk entitled 'How doctors can do more good', but I was intrigued.

I'd never really questioned the positive impact of doctors before then. I'd always thought it was a given that medicine is a great career because you save loads of lives. Yet this talk suggested that it wasn't quite that simple.

Conventional wisdom is that the ultimate role of a doctor is to be as competent as possible. As long as a doctor is competent, they are doing a good job. While learning the academic and clinical aspects of medicine, as outlined in Chapters 2 and 3, are of fundamental importance, there are reasons why a doctor in the 21st century should be aiming to do much more than that. This chapter explores why and how.

Why should we do more?

Medicine = mostly algorithms

There are optimum algorithms to follow in almost all situations, as determined by the existing evidence base and 'best practice'. It is how well a doctor follows these algorithms which determines the impact they have in their clinical practice. Skills such as communication and teamwork are important but their impact may be less direct.

Becoming a better medical student and doctor involves becoming better at these algorithms. Early on we learn the algorithms for taking a history and doing examinations. We learn the algorithms for treating different conditions. Examples include the 'Acute Coronary Syndrome (ACS) protocol' for the immediate response to a heart attack or the 'GOLD guidelines' for long-term management of COPD.

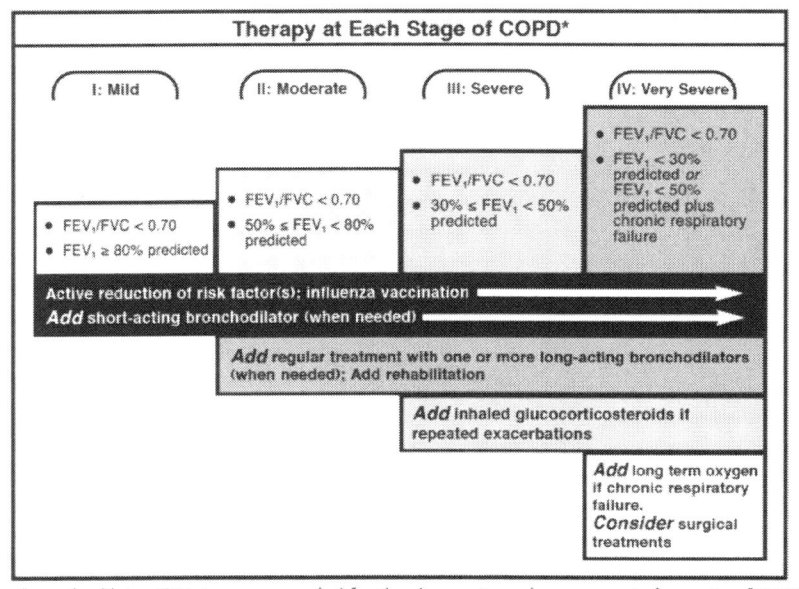

Therapy at Each Stage of COPD*				
	I: Mild	II: Moderate	III: Severe	IV: Very Severe
	$FEV_1/FVC < 0.70$ $FEV_1 \geq 80\%$ predicted	$FEV_1/FVC < 0.70$ $50\% \leq FEV_1 < 80\%$ predicted	$FEV_1/FVC < 0.70$ $30\% \leq FEV_1 < 50\%$ predicted	$FEV_1/FVC < 0.70$ $FEV_1 < 30\%$ predicted or $FEV_1 < 50\%$ predicted plus chronic respiratory failure
Active reduction of risk factor(s); influenza vaccination				→
Add short-acting bronchodilator (when needed)				→
		Add regular treatment with one or more long-acting bronchodilators (when needed); Add rehabilitation		
			Add inhaled glucocorticosteroids if repeated exacerbations	
				Add long term oxygen if chronic respiratory failure. *Consider* surgical treatments

*Postbronchodilator FEV_1 is recommended for the diagnosis and assessment of severity of COPD.

Diminishing returns

Ongoing medical training is aimed at increasing the ability to follow these algorithms. More skilled doctors are able to follow them more consistently and more quickly. They also have a greater appreciation of the intricacies of the algorithms.

All medically-qualified doctors are, by definition, considered competent. They are deemed good enough at following the required protocols in order treat their patients.

The benefits of exerting effort to further exceed this 'competency threshold' are subject to the law of diminishing returns, as shown below.

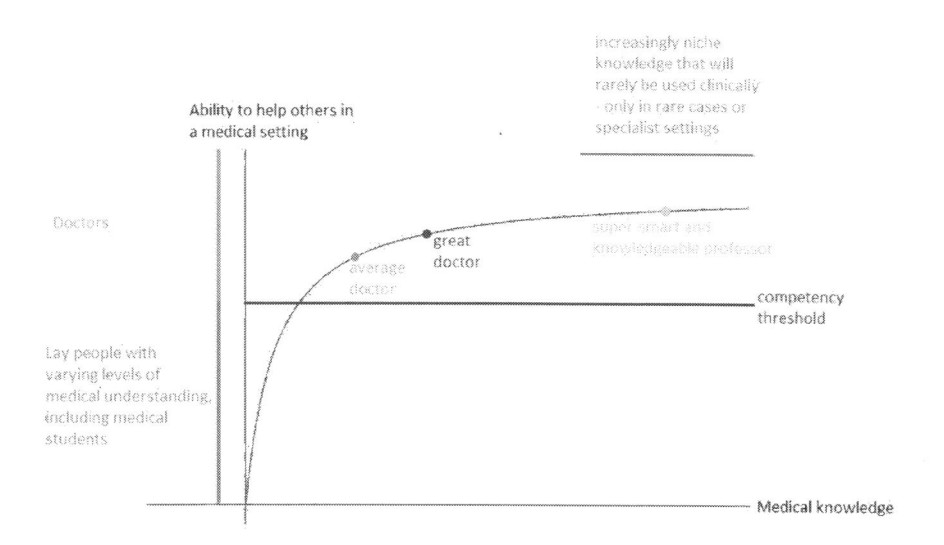

Greater understanding of medicine beyond what is required for competency does not lead to a significantly better impact on patients for a number of reasons:

There is extensive guidance on the different algorithms to follow, including NICE guidelines, trust guidelines and other resources.

If you are unsure of an action, more often than not specific guidelines will exist that you can follow.

Greater knowledge doesn't necessarily lead to better action. For example, someone may know that NSAIDs should not be used in a patient with asthma because inhibiting COX enzymes leads to an increase in leukotriene levels which exacerbates asthma. However, another person can know only 'don't use NSAIDs in asthma' and will still be able to take the same action.

As a junior doctor, you can consult senior doctors if unsure. If a decision is outside of your scope, a senior or a specialist will be able to help.

As a senior doctor, you can consult people with more specialist experience. When something falls outside of your clinical comfort zone, there are other doctors with more experience in that particular area that can help.

Treating the patients you meet

The benefits of the competent-to-excellent progression faces a further restriction; you can only treat the patients directly in front of you. You are only one individual so no matter how much better you may be than your peers at clinical medicine, only the patients fortunate enough to interact with you directly will benefit from this.

This is not the case in other fields or professions. For example, consider the public health researcher who devises a scheme that lowers the national smoking rate or the researcher who contributes to the discovery of a new anti-cancer drug. Even a relatively tiny contribution can lead to greater overall benefits due to the ability to scale up. For a population of 50,000, would you rather have 1 amazing doctor or 100 average doctors? How about 1 amazing scientist or 100 average scientists? These answers are different for a reason.

Therefore, the doctors who make the greatest positive contribution to the health of a population do so through things which can scale-up and affect more people. There are approaches that can be taken at medical school to maximise our ability of doing so.

How can we increase our impact?

In the talk referenced at the start of this chapter, entitled 'How doctors can do more good', Dr Gregory Lewis presented evidence suggesting that a banker giving away 10% of his earnings to cost-effective charities will save more lives (measured as QALYs or Quality-Adjusted Life Years) than the average doctor. (Of course, the average banker doesn't give away 10% of his earnings to charity.)

In this book I will explore instead how we can increase our positive impact directly through our work. For those interested in Dr Lewis' work, he explains the research in depth on the 80,000 Hours blog: https://80000hours.org/2012/08/how-many-lives-does-a-doctor-save/

Extending our work beyond our direct clinical practice can dramatically enhance our positive impact. Doing so requires motivation so it needs to be something that we enjoy. Therefore, one of the best ways to maximise our contribution to the medical field is to find something we love doing and work out how to use it to make a positive impact.

Based on our unique combination of genetic make-up and personal experiences there are certain areas we are predisposed to enjoy and excel in. However, discovering these areas can involve a lot of hard work. Cal Newport is a computer science professor who researched the pursuit of fulfilling work. He found that you must develop a sufficient level of skill and insight to know whether you deeply enjoy an area[7]. This requires a sustained period of hard work.

There is no one-size-fits-all approach to finding what we love. It often involves a wide exploration and a lot of trial-and-error. However, two principles that can facilitate it are **undertaking extensive self-education** and **developing fundamental transferrable skills**. I shall explore these principles in this chapter as well as Chapters 5 and 6.

Medical school provides a great opportunity to do so. We have more free time, fewer real-life commitments and more opportunities for experimentation.

The benefits of extending our work

Finding work you love can provide you with immense satisfaction as well as maximise the impact you have.

In the short-term, pleasure and drive gained from working hard towards something you love has knock-on effects in other areas of your life. By increasing your mood and your drive it can lead to better performance in clinical practice. It also gives you motivation to study efficiently to make more time for what you love.

---

[7] Newport, *So Good They Can't Ignore You*.

In the long-term, the greater levels of skill and understanding that can be attained will maximise your ability to make a positive impact on the medical field. You may think of improvements or find solutions that have never been found before. The ways that this can be done are extremely broad so I will demonstrate with some examples. These are far from comprehensive.

Incorporating our passion into medicine

Some people will find deep interest in areas that can combine with medicine quite naturally, enabling them to have a positive impact.

Mr Samer Nashef is a prominent cardiac surgeon who combined an interest in statistics with his medical expertise to create a risk model for cardiac surgery called the EuroSCORE. This has been implemented world-wide and can be credited with saving millions of lives by improving success rates and reducing unnecessary surgery.

Mr Shafi Ahmed is a surgeon who is interested in novel technology and in medical education. He combined these interests by live-streaming operations by wearing special glasses which record what he can see. He gave teaching while conducting these operations and they have been watched by thousands in the comfort of their own homes. He has founded Medical Realities which uses virtual reality and augmented reality to improve surgical training.

For others, the potential for combination may not be as obvious.

Mandeep Singh is a medical student whose passion is learning to rap. For a long time, medicine and rap were two very separate parts of his life. Then he decided to use rapping as a medium to help patients and to improve healthcare. One way is to tell stories which can help patients process certain emotions and psychological problems. He played me one of his raps describing the experiences of a patient he'd met, and it almost brought me to tears. He has written an insightful account of principles for developing mastery in rap but which are transferrable to other areas also: https://chrislovejoy.me/rap/.

When exploring personal interests, try to avoid filtering things out based on how easily they may be applied to medicine. It's better to explore things you are more genuinely passionate about, even if you have to work harder to incorporate it into medicine at a later date. Sometimes the potential for combining interests will not be obvious until higher levels of mastery are obtained.

It is possible, however, that you may find a passion in something that you deem incompatible with medicine. While you may be content to keep it as a hobby, the enjoyment may drive you to make it a bigger feature of your life. This presents you with a tough decision. It may be that medicine prevents you from doing the things that provide the deepest enjoyment and satisfaction. If this is case, then the right decision may be to follow your passion rather than stay in medicine wishing you were elsewhere. If you ever question whether medicine is right for you, I consider this question in greater depth in the chapter "Is Medicine Right For Me?".

There is no way to guarantee that you will find work you love. Everyone's path in life is different. However, two fundamental things that can enable you to discover deeper levels of enjoyment and satisfaction are **self-education**, which I will explore now, and **developing fundamental transferrable skills,** which I will explore in Chapters 5 and 6.

Self-Education: the 21st Century Super-Power

Self-education enables us to develop the understanding required for insight into our enjoyment of a particular area. Recent technological advances, such as the internet and mobile devices, now provide unprecedented potential for high-level self-education.

Once you start to yield the rewards of doing so, it is like continuing down a metaphorical rabbit hole. After learning about one area, it will open up new areas and possibilities and each time you can select the next route based on your personal inclinations. The deeper you go, the greater the depths of interest you develop and the more 'passion' you can find.

The first step is to identify what your potential areas of interest are. This can take any form; a subject area, a skill, an artform. Don't limit yourself to something that must be obviously related to medicine. You must then actively work to develop expertise in the area. At a fundamental level, an approach for doing so is to:

1. Identify good sources of input and methods of output.
2. Incorporate them into daily life.

Identifying good sources of input and methods of output

The three main domains by which we can learn are by auditory input, visual input and by output (thinking, making and doing).

The ratio of different types of input and output depends on the area that you select. For example, if, as Mandeep, you want to learn to rap, then output is of utmost importance but you would also want to spend time listening to other rappers (auditory input). Reading (visual input) would be of less importance. If you wanted to learn academic content, the ratio may be more evenly spread.

You can also match the ratios to your personal preferences. I learn much better from auditory input so will prioritise an audiobook over visual reading where possible. Most commonly, a balance of different types is the best approach.

Auditory input includes audiobooks, YouTube videos and podcasts. Great sources of audiobooks include Audible (paid), LibroVox and Project Gutenberg (both free). I've heard there may even be pirate-themed websites where you can download audiobooks that other people have shared (though only if there is no copyright, so it is useful for old books). There is software that enables you to download YouTube videos (for personal use only) and one source of great podcasts is the TuneIn Radio app.

Visual input includes reading books and blogs. UsedBookSearch.co.uk is a great website for finding cheap second-hand books (often as cheap as £0.01 + £2.80 delivery). While buying lots of books may seem expensive, I would argue that a good book can change the way you see the world so may be the most cost-effective investment you can make. There are a huge number of blogs out there so try to find the best ones to suit your purpose.

Output is an essential stage in all learning. It may involve writing about something you're learning; manipulating information that you have come across or forming your own opinions can highlight gaps in your knowledge and consolidate ideas. It may involve teaching others. It helps avoid the trap of thinking that because you have read X number of books on a subject, you are automatically an expert. You must also grapple with the content to ensure you understand the ideas. Alternatively, it may involve practising the skill, such as writing raps in the case of Mandeep.

Think about your area of interest and what type of output can help you to master it. Are you learning lots of complex ideas? If so, how could you consolidate them. Are you developing a skill? If so, how could you practise it. For example, you could write a blog, start a podcast or start a project – it is specific to your area, so you can be creative.

Incorporating them into daily life

Our day provides a plethora of opportunities for different forms of information input or output. There will be gaps in your day when you could read something. There will be activities that you do regularly, during which you could listen to something. There will be certain times of day optimum for creating something.

Go through your typical day or week from beginning to end and see where you could incorporate learning. For example, at times I was commuting 30 mins to medical placement and back so I listened to audiobooks. In the mornings, my mind often wanders while I eat breakfast so I started recalling information or brainstorming ideas while I ate.

I would recommend developing these new habits gradually, as taking on new tasks can be cognitively straining. But your brain will adapt and they will become easier with time, until you no longer have to think about it.

It's useful to set targets and deadlines. For example, I often do one-month projects where I do something, such as writing a blog post or reading a book, every day. I also set the personal target of reading 100 books every year.

However, it's easy to set over-ambitious targets. Therefore, it's important to objectively assess your past track-record and set gradually increasing targets. Smart small, until it's comfortable, then increase.

After maintaining this approach for a period of time, you will hit a point of positive feedback. You will start to see tangible rewards for your efforts, which feeds back as further motivation for learning. For example, after investing time and effort into blogging, I started to get positive feedback and build up an audience – this excitement gave me the motivation to wake up early and write blog posts before starting work. At some point, you will hit a point of no return where you are fully committed to finding passionate work and you won't want to go back to your previous lifestyle.

For more information about this system, as well as how to transition up and down a "hierarchy" of inputs and outputs based on your circumstance, check out the following post on my blog: http://chrislovejoy.co.uk/free-moments/.

The benefits of self-education

The gains from this approach extend well beyond the content that you learn. It increases your ability to retain further information and to come up with new ideas.

The Velcro Theory of Memory compares retaining information to Velcro; the more 'hooks' (previously understood concepts) you have for the loops (new information) to hold onto, the more likely it is to stick.

James Altucher is a best-selling author and entrepreneur who advises people to, each day, read for at least an hour and to write out ten new ideas. He says that the more ideas you have in your head, the better the ideas you will produce. He describes this phenomenon as 'idea sex'; the ideas in your head will combine and, akin to sexual reproduction, will produce offspring ideas which can be even better.

We are entering an era with an unprecedented rate of change. The rate of technological advancement is increasing exponentially. The future belongs to those who are the most adaptable and the ability to extensively self-educate will be an increasingly important skill.

The field of medicine is slow to adapt to these changes and embrace new possibilities. It is for this reason that I started the Future Doctors, which is a network of ambitious doctors determined to make a difference to medicine and to the world. Through sharing advice, experiences and resources we want to help each other make an impact. If this sounds like something that would interest you, visit www.FutureDoctors.co.

Developing fundamental transferrable skills

Self-education, as described in this chapter, can be applied to medicine or any other field. There are other ways, for which opportunities exist at medical school, to develop skills which will maximise the impact you have and your ability to find an area you love.

The ability to think well and communicate well, both orally and through writing, are fundamental transferrable skills. They can help in many areas of life as a doctor and beyond. Developing these abilities can be enjoyable in their own right. In Chapter 5, I will explore how scientific research can be used to increase your ability to think well. In Chapter 6, I will explore how writing and teaching can increase your ability to communicate well and outline the opportunities for doing so at medical school.

~~~

MEDICAL STUDENT CHALLENGE 1: Self-educate in a topic that interests you. Set a goal to work towards and a deadline for achieving it. *Example goals: Write a 4,000 word essay, read 10 books on the subject, publish an original research article in the area.*

~~~

CHAPTER 4 SUMMARY

- The competency of a doctor is primarily determined by how well they can follow medical algorithms.
- We can only treat the patients we meet. This limits the positive impact that improving our clinical practice can have.
- We can enhance our impact by making progress in an area of medicine that can scale up.
- The best way to do so is to find something we love and incorporate it into improving medicine.
- To maximise our chance of finding something we love and making an impact, we can self-educate and develop fundamental transferrable skills.

- Self-education involves selecting an area, identifying good sources of information and incorporating learning into your daily life.
- The world is changing faster than ever so learning to be adaptable is invaluable.

Chapter 5: A Scientific Approach to Research

I turned off my computer, flicked the light switch and climbed into bed. I was bored and exhausted.

I'd used up all my motivational reserves over the last three hours, trudging through excel data on my computer. I didn't even see why this project was important. It wasn't clear to me how it would help anyone, patients or doctors.

'Well, at least I'll get a paper published', I thought.

A long story, short: that paper was never published. Bummer.

Fast-forward two years and the enthusiasm with which I clicked the 'Submit' button was almost palpable.

I'd spent far more late nights on this project than the first one, but I didn't mind.

Three weeks later, when I received the email that began "It is a pleasure to accept your manuscript in its current form", I pumped my fists into the air with jubilation.

~~~

Medical school offers many opportunities to get involved in research. You can do it alongside placements or during your holidays.

Should you get involved in research? What's the best approach? Let's explore the answers to these questions.

Do your own work

Learning to think for yourself is one of the most valuable skills you can develop. Scientific research can be a great arena for developing this ability but only if the right approach is taken. It can also directly help your medical career as published scientific papers strengthen future job applications and can help you to establish connections.

Progress in scientific understanding is fuelled by new ideas. Those that contribute most to science are those with the ability to think most clearly to come up with new ideas. We often create an us-them distinction between 'geniuses' who come up with great ideas and the 'normal' rest of us who can only marvel at them. Yet this ability can be improved by taking an intelligent approach for a sustained period. The approach to self-education described in Chapter 4 and the learning for understanding principle outlined in Chapter 2 can be a part of this development.

The most common approach to scientific research as a student does little to foster this ability. It involves taking on a pre-formed project from a senior doctor or researcher and giving up your time to do the boring parts of the project. By crunching the numbers or sifting through the data, you will get your name on the final paper.

However, you gain little else as the 'higher thinking' parts of the project (conception, study design and analysis) have already been completed. At most, you will gain some insight into the thought process of the actual scientist behind the study and it may also stimulate some thought of your own regarding other possible projects or ways the data may be interpreted. It is a very inefficient way to develop the ability to think well and involves giving away valuable free time purely for CV points. This may only be justified if you are applying for a super-competitive specialty and need your name on as many papers as possible. Even then, it may become more efficient to conceive ideas and have someone else do the leg-work once you have developed your ability to think of good project ideas.

In short, the approach to take is think of your project idea first and then find the most suitable supervisor based on the idea.

The idea

We must learn to think for ourselves and train our brains to come up with good ideas. Active brainstorming is to our brains what regular exercise is to our bodies. Below I've outlined a useful approach to brainstorming. However, while the technique is simple and effective, the act of doing so regularly can be challenging.

One reason is that we typically don't value our ideas highly enough. When confronted with a problem, many seek someone else to provide us with an answer. Another is the discipline it takes. Trying to think deeply on any subject strains our brains and it can be frustrating if we don't see early positive results. The easy route out is to distract ourselves or let our minds wander. It is only through continuous trial and error that our thinking ability will improve.

In combination, these issues may prevent us from trying to think deeply in order to solve problems. Without practice, our ideas may not be good so we take the answers from others and thus never get the practice required.

One idea can change the world. Every Nobel Prize started out as an idea. To give ourselves the best chance of coming up with ideas that will improve our lives and the lives of those around us, we must train our brains to do so. Actively brainstorming is a way to start this process. In his book Deep Work, Cal Newport explains ways to go further.

If you are interested in the principles behind thinking for ourselves and improving the world, Tim Urban has written an excellent piece using Elon Musk to demonstrate how to do so and addressing the issues of pride, fear and the influence of society:
https://waitbutwhy.com/2015/11/the-cook-and-the-chef-musks-secret-sauce.html

Active brainstorming

1. Create the right environment

Block out a period of at least an hour. Remove all distractions during this time. For me, this means phone in another room, computer switched off and ensuring I won't be interrupted by friends.

2. Get ready

Sit down with a sheet of paper, a pen and nothing else. In theory, a computer, phone or tablet would be fine to write on but make sure you won't get any notifications or other distractions.

Decide the topic or question that you will brainstorm on.

3. **Think of as many ideas as possible**

As soon as you think of an idea, write it down. It doesn't matter if you feel it's terrible. Any bad idea may lead to a good idea plus no-one else is going to read it (unless you take a photo of it and put it in a book…). Don't try to filter your ideas at this stage as it will disrupt your creative flow.

If the ideas don't come easily, persevere. Don't allow yourself to get distracted or quit. It's easy to give up when you feel resistance but commit to at least one hour focussed on the task.

If the ideas do start to flow, keep asking follow-up questions, considering different variations or combinations of the ideas you come up with.

4. **Filter the ideas**

Once you have exhausted all lines of exploration or are feeling mentally 'spent', it's time to go back and assess what you've come up with.

Which ideas have the greatest potential? If you could only keep three, which would they be? Which ideas seem bad at first glance but may be modified in some way? You can brainstorm further if new ideas start to form.

5. **Test the ideas**

Discuss the idea with a friend who will ask you probing questions. Practise articulating the concept so you know exactly what it is that you've come up with. A friend may highlight positive or negative aspects that you didn't think of.

Search the internet to see if anyone has had this idea before or anything similar. Part of you may not want to know if it already exists but make sure your search is thorough. You don't want to put in work only to later realise it has already been done. However, if you see something similar don't readily dismiss your idea as there may be a fundamental distinction.

For a scientific research project idea, undertake an extensive literature search. Use PubMed to do a focussed search of existing studies in a similar manner to above. Having seen what other people have done, what new ideas can you think of related to your idea or theirs?

If your idea is for an entrepreneurial pursuit, Josh Kaufman has provided an excellent checklist of "Ten Ways to Evaluate a Market" which are available here: https://personalmba.com/10-ways-to-evaluate-a-market/.

~~~

Note: The main limitation is not finding the time to do this. Put this book down right now and have a brainstorm. Remove distractions, grab some paper, decide an area of medicine you want to think about and give it a go!

I'd be interested to hear about any benefit you get from this method or any new ideas you come up with. I'm also happy to be the friend who objectively assesses your idea. Drop me an email and I'll help in any way I can: chris@medicalstudentmanual.com.

~~~

Pain points in healthcare

For example, one evening I brainstormed on 'Pain points in healthcare'. I have attached images of the original notes below. (Excuse the bad handwriting... doctor in training.)

Most of the routes of exploration did not produce anything of value. However, from this brainstorm I came up with two good ideas which myself and a colleague worked on.

In the process of finding these two good ideas, there were many bad ideas and failed routes of inquiry. These is just part of the process. I have circled them in red and explained why they are bad ideas below.

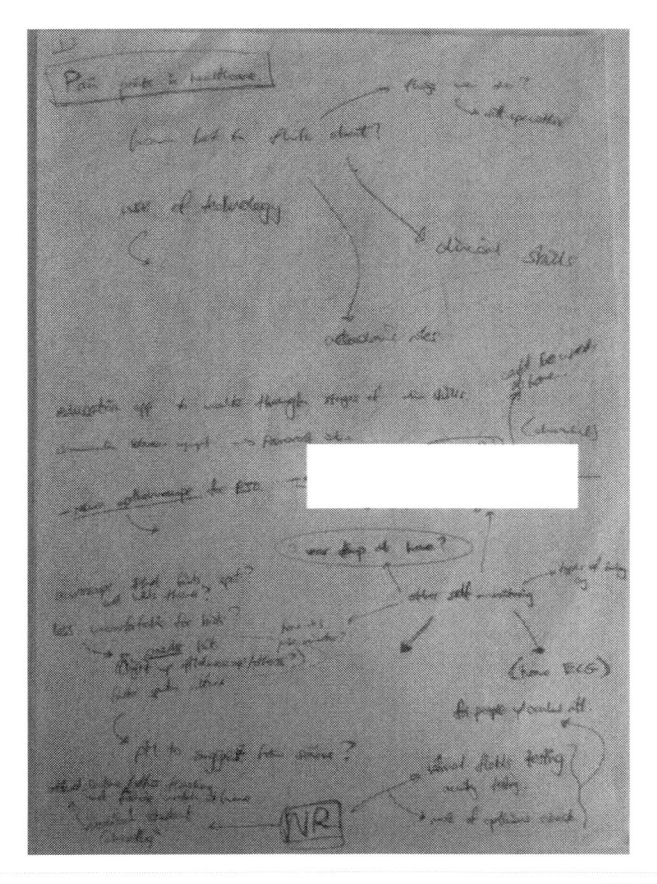

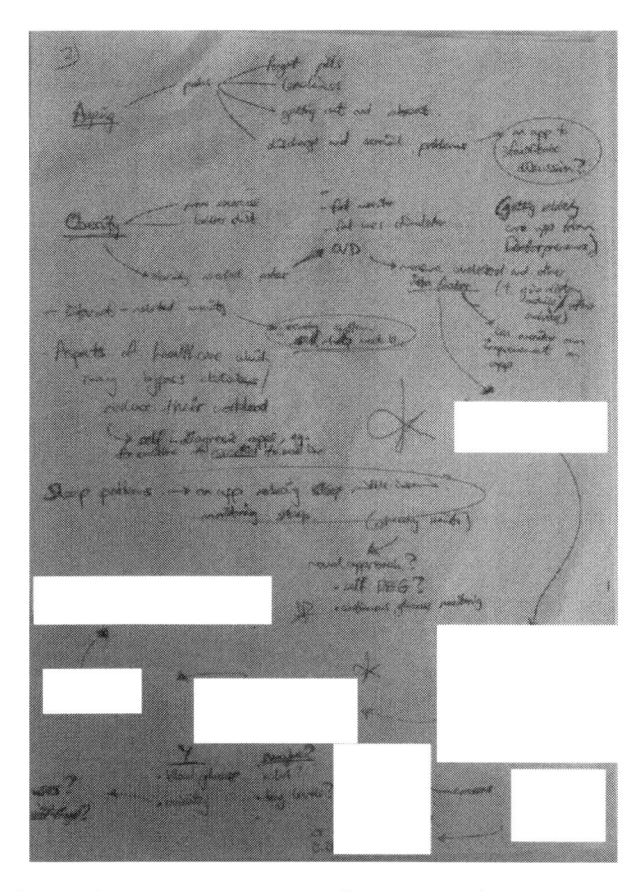

1. Measuring temperature at home via the ear: parents already often measure their children's temperatures when they get ill.
2. A stethoscope that lights up or makes sounds to distract babies: adding lights or sounds to a stethoscope would be highly impractical and offers little benefit on top of having a stethoscope and a toy that lights up or makes sounds separately.
3. Creating an app to facilitate discharge discussion would be highly challenging and not possible for someone who isn't already well-integrated in healthcare management.
4. CBT self-help modules for anxiety already exist.
5. Apps that monitor sleep quality already exist.

The supervisor

As a student, you will need a supervisor on board for the project. They will be able to provide you feedback throughout the project, know-how about the publication process and may be required for certain applications (such as ethical clearance for studies involving patients).

Choosing the supervisor

The supervisor you choose can have a major impact on the quality of your project so it is worth investing a significant amount of time finding the right one. The ideal supervisor is someone with relevant experience of the field your study is in, a good record of publishing papers and who will be able to find the time to give you regular feedback and help with challenges that arise. There is really nothing more valuable than feedback from your supervisor at every stage of the process.

For the first two points, it is worth doing an extensive background search on the internet including PubMed. See how often they are publishing papers, in which journals and what research questions they are trying to answer. For the third point, the best source of information is people who have previously done projects with them. Do you know anybody, or is there anyone who could put you in touch with somebody?

It would be useful if your supervisor is in your area, so that you can meet face-to-face, but this is not essential; discussions via email and/or skype can be adequate.

Contacting the supervisor

Contacting a renowned scientist to pitch your project idea can be daunting but it's important not to be put off. Most researchers would love the prospect of an enthusiastic student pitching them ideas.

Two ways to contact a potential supervisor are face-to-face or by email. Face-to-face relies on them being in your location. If you know they are giving a talk, pay attention to the talk and ask questions at the end. Then go and speak to them about your idea. If they work at a nearby hospital, go to the hospital and find their office or a ward or clinic they are working at and ask to meet them. Be prepared to be told to come back another day or to book an appointment. This may seem daunting, but good things come to those that push their comfort zone.

If contacting via email, I would advise including a personalised introduction to get their attention and let them know you are serious. For example, "I was reading about your work on…", "I read your book about… and thought…". Try and link it into the rest of the email, which should include a succinct description of your project, it's purpose, what you hope to achieve and what you want them to help with.

Most importantly, keep trying. You may have to contact a lot of people but don't be put off. Krtin Nithiyanandam was fifteen years old when he contacted over a hundred labs. He was rejected but almost all of them, but ended up discovering a new diagnostic test for Alzheimer's Disease.

Here are two example emails that I have used to secure projects:

Email 1

Here I had a specific project in mind and a specific doctor who I hoped would act as the project lead.

Dear Dr ____,

I am a Cambridge medical student with a project idea related to *(specialty)*. I am currently looking for a project lead and would be interested in meeting to discuss this with you.

My project idea is to _____. This would involve:
- Compiling a database of _____ (this will require ethical approval)
- Training a neural network to _____ (this will involve some consultant consensus)

Correspondingly, our main requirements from a project lead would be help with:
- Attaining ethical approval
- Assisting with data collection for the database
- Provided consensus on the _____

Our aim is to _____, with potential use in education and clinical practice.

Would you be happy to meet to discuss the project further? If not, could you recommend other clinicians who may be interested in being our project lead?

Kind regards,
Chris Lovejoy

Email 2

In this case, I had a few project ideas rather than a specific project and was more focussed on doing a project with a particular doctor.

Dear Dr _____,

I am a fifth year Cambridge medical student who recently completed my rotation at _____ Hospital, during which time I attended your teaching – you may remember me as the student who brought your book to the teaching.

I greatly enjoyed reading your book and I share your desire to contribute to the improvement of healthcare provision, as well as possessing an interest in _____. From _____ until _____ this year I will be undertaking my SSC and I would love to work with you to better understand how I can increase my contribution to the medical field and to gain more experience in _____. I am enthusiastic, ambitious and willing to invest large amounts of time and effort both inside and outside the hospital.

Kind regards,
Chris Lovejoy

Writing the paper

A good supervisor will give advice on what information to include in each section. There are also many useful guides available on the internet.

One short and well-written article which is a great introduction for writing your first paper is http://www.liebertpub.com/media/pdf/English-Research-Article-Writing-Guide.pdf. It outlines what should be written in each section and suggests the best order to write them in.

A more detailed guide is available on PubMed here: https://www.ncbi.nlm.nih.gov/pmc/articles/PMC3474301/.

~~~

MEDICAL STUDENT CHALLENGE 2: Undertake at least one research project based on an idea that you come up with.

~~~

CHAPTER 5 SUMMARY

- Developing the ability to think well can benefit your own life and the lives of those around you.
- Scientific research can help you develop this ability if you think of your own ideas and undergo continual trial-and-error.
- Active brainstorming is a useful way to think of new ideas to use in scientific research or elsewhere.
- Finding a good supervisor is important. It can be hard but persistence and strategy is important.

Chapter 6: Commanding Clearer Communication

"The scan showed it is something sinister", the consultant explained. "We think probably the best is to let you be."

The lack of comprehension was evident on the elderly gentleman's face.

"Alright." The consultant said, as he got up and left the room.

The patient had metastatic gastric cancer. He had been discussed in the gastroenterology MDT (multi-disciplinary team) meeting the previous day. Based on the severity of the cancer and its widespread dissemination throughout the patient's body, they had decided that surgery was futile.

I knew this, but the patient didn't. And I didn't feel that the consultant's explanation had made it any clearer.

I was the only other member on the team that day. It was up to me. If I didn't go back and explain the diagnosis and options going forward, the patient would be anxious and confused for days.

I went back at the end of the ward round. The patient's family were now present, also anxious and confused. It was still my first month on the job. This was going to be challenging…

~~~

The ability to communicate well, through writing and orally, are fundamental transferrable skills which can help in medicine and other areas of life. They can also be enjoyable in their own right. Oral communication is important, as demonstrated above. Interaction with patients is a major part of practising medicine and can often be challenging. Good team work also relies on effective communication. Within medicine, writing is an important medium for sharing ideas both within the medical community and with members of the public.

One of the best ways to develop oral communication at medical school is through teaching. You must explain things in ways that other people will understand and adjust your explanation to the audience. This is also the case when you explain things to patients, communicate with other medical professionals and even to explain things to yourself. Other benefits include consolidating your learning (there is nothing like an eager student asking probing questions to test your own understanding) and the opportunity to earn money. Other ways to develop oral communication include public speaking and debating.

The best way to develop writing skill is through goal-orientated writing and feedback. Ways to obtain this as a medical student include essay prizes, writing freelance articles and blogging. Other benefits include the possibility of contributing to others with what you write, earning money and CV points plus unexpected opportunities.

Oral communication in healthcare

Developing the ability to communicate well with patients, relatives and other members of the team is an important part of becoming a great doctor. Communication can even have an impact on patient outcomes. Danielle Ofri describes the following study in her book "What Patients Say, What Doctors Hear":

'A group of about 100 patients undergoing abdominal surgery were studied. The night before the operation, the anaesthetist visited each patient to explain the surgery and anaesthesia. For half the patients (randomly selected), the anaesthetists added in a twenty-minute discussion about post-op pain. Patients were told that pain was a normal part of the process and that it was caused by muscle spasms. They were told where the pain would likely be located, when to expect it and how long it would last...

... The group with the extra discussion needed half the amount of pain relief medication that the control group needed. The real shocker was that these patients were discharged from hospital 3 days earlier than those in the control group. A typical day in hospital costs more than $4,000 dollars, so this was a decidedly low-tech intervention that saved more than $12,000 dollars and spared patients many days of pain and misery.'

However, as a medical student the opportunities to develop effective communication skills directly are limited. There are limits to how much can be learnt through observation and simulation.

You won't be asked to discuss with occupational therapists or physiotherapists about whether a patient can be discharged. You won't be asked to update family members on a patient's progress since admission. You won't be asked to inform a patient of their cancer diagnosis. Once qualified, you will be asked to do all the above and much more.

The transition from medical school to qualified doctor requires you to adapt and no amount of preparation at medical school will stop this from being the case. However, there are approaches that can be taken at medical school which will make the communication aspect of this transition smoother. Broadly, this involves improving both general and medicine-specific communication ability.

General ability can be developed through any activity which involves conscious effort towards good communication. One of the best ways to develop oral communication at medical school is through teaching, which I will explore in depth in this chapter. Other examples are debating and public speaking, which can also increase clarity and confidence.

Medicine-specific communication skills are often directly taught as part of the medical course. They include sessions on 'history-taking' or 'explanation and planning' which may involve practising with actors or with real patients. Learning these skills in isolation is an example of the deconstructing skills approach outlined in Chapter 3. It is important to get practice integrating these skills, although for the reasons described earlier this can be difficult as a student. Despite the limitations described above, get as much practice as possible by proactively talking to patients and other members of the healthcare team.

The greater the level of competence achieved in these skills, the easier it will be to transition from being a student to being a qualified doctor.

~~~

Learning Through Observation

Although it is not possible to fully learn a skill without doing it, a lot can be learnt from active observation. An excellent GP gave me the following advice:

"Find a good role model. Observe them; what is it that they say? What is it that they do? Little things can make a huge difference. Notice doctors that make you think 'I never want to be like that'; What is it that they said and did which had a negative impact on patients?"

~~~

Further resources

For further reading about communication in healthcare, see the following:

What Patients Say, What Doctors Hear by Danielle Ofri uses real-life stories to explore of the challenges of doctor-patient communication and considers how we can overcome them.

Skills for Communicating with Patients by Jonathan Silverman is a more systematic, textbook-style approach to learning communication skills for people who want to delve deeper into the theory.

Learning to teach well

As well as helping you to develop good oral communication, teaching others is an important role of a doctor. As a medical student, you depend on doctors for many aspects of your medical education and it won't be long before you are in their position teaching students and doctors more junior than you.

I remember the anxiety I initially felt at the prospect of having my knowledge probed by intelligent and inquisitive students. What if they asked me a question I couldn't answer? What if I suddenly forgot everything I was going to say? You may have similar fears but remember that doing anything outside your comfort zone stretches you as a person. With practice, this anxiety will reduce.

Regardless how you feel about teaching, I would highly recommend gaining at least ten hours of contact-time. Ten hours will enable you to understand the format, overcome initial anxieties and start to develop your own style. This will give you a greater appreciation of whether it is for you.

One easy way to acquire ten hours of experience is by finding a student to tutor. I consider the practicalities of this below. However, there are many alternatives, from teaching groups of medical students to volunteering at a local school.

You may find a passion for teaching after overcoming the initial anxiety as I did. Even if you don't, you will have expanded your comfort zone, gained some teaching skill and earned some money at the same time.

Becoming a Tutor

What should I tutor?

The two most common things to tutor are academic subjects (such as GCSEs or A-Levels) or tutoring for university medical admissions (UKCAT or BMAT, interview preparation and other parts of the application). You could also teach a skill, such as playing a musical instrument, chess or a sport. For initial teaching experience, I would encourage starting with GCSE or below or an admissions test that you performed well on.

Finding students

There are many different ways to go about finding students. The easiest way is to sign up for a tutoring agency to advertise your services. The downside of this is they will take a cut (typically 10-20%).

I won't list websites here as it is location-dependent and I don't want to endorse any particular organisations. However, there are stacks of companies for tutoring subjects or for tutoring medical admissions.

The alternative is to advertise yourself. You can do this via the internet with a personal website or through a freelancing agency. Again, there are loads of websites for doing so which are also location-dependent.

You can also do it in person. Opportunities may be available with the friends of relatives or friend's friends. Think about people you know of the appropriate age/subject and enquire. You can also advertise your services in the local area.

Further resources

If you are interested in teaching, two good books on this subject are:

Surely You're Joking, Mr Feynman, which is a collection of entertaining short stories about Richard Feynman, widely regarded as one of the best physicists and best teachers of the 20th century. Many great insights about teaching are scattered throughout the book.

Teaching What You Don't Know by Therese Huston, in which the author draws on experience teaching university students to tackle common problems such as what to do when you don't have a clue how to answer a question.

Learning to write well

Some people find writing comes more naturally than others. However, writing ability is something that can be learnt. Doing so also increases clarity of thought more broadly. I always struggled with writing but, after hard work over many years, have reached the point where I can write this book. If you have made it this far in the book, I must at least be doing something right!

Essay prizes

Essay prizes offer a fantastic opportunity to develop writing ability, gain CV points and make money all at the same time. All the different medical specialties are very keen to encourage students to consider their area in depth, hoping to entice them to choose it later down the line, and thus many offer healthily-sized financial prizes. There are many prizes available and some receive low numbers of applicants.

Finding an essay

There are essay prizes on a wide variety of topics. I would advise thinking firstly of your interests and then finding an essay asking a question you would be interested in knowing the answer to. This provides the organic motivation required to push through difficulty of writing the essay.

To find niche essay titles that are in an area of your personal interest, I would suggest searching that area along with some variation of 'medical student prize/essay/competition'.

For example, after reading a lot of science fiction I wanted to write a science fiction short story related to medicine and managed to find a competition run by the University of Glasgow (but open to everybody): http://scifimedhums.glasgow.ac.uk/writing-competition/.

Many essay prizes are not particularly well advertised but can be found in the hidden recesses of the internet so it's well worth doing a thorough search.

Useful websites to check out for essay titles:

- The Royal Society of Medicine have loads of essay prizes in all different specialities: https://www.rsm.ac.uk/prizes-awards/students.aspx
- Your university is likely to have some (and here the potential pool of applicants is much smaller)
- Specific specialties and their associated societies

Alternatives to essays

An alternative way to write and make money as a medical student is writing **freelance articles** for websites or other medical outlets. I dabbled in this but felt restricted by some of the restraints, such as having to write on specific topics. If you are interested here is a great guide about how to get into it:

https://blog.freelancersunion.org/2014/09/10/how-to-start-freelance-writer/

If you think writing may be a significant part of your future career, freelance writing offers the advantage of providing a portfolio of work which can help to secure future employment.

Starting an **internet blog** is another alternative. It may not offer the same CV points or financial gain but it does offer the freedom to write about whatever is on your mind. It can also play a role in self-education, as outlined in Chapter 4. There are also rewards that you can't really predict. For example, after one post someone approached me asking to collaborate on a project and after another the editor of an online magazine requested to feature it.

Writing for scientific journals is another great way to hone skills and support future applications. This is one part of undertaking your own research, as discussed in Chapter 5. However, there are many alternatives, such as literature reviews (where you summarise research in an area of interest), perspective pieces (where you give an opinion) and case studies (about interesting patients).

Principles for improvement

1. **Get started**

It sounds obvious but this can be the hardest step.

It took me a long time to get started with writing. The perfectionist within me wanted to capture everything perfectly yet I could never find the right words. I remember countless hours at school trying to write essays or short stories and just looking at a blank page, not able to start.

It can be difficult to accept that your writing is not as good as you want it to be. You may have your heart set on winning an essay prize and worry that you'll work hard and have nothing to show for it.

However, it's important to accept that you may well not win and be happy to write it regardless. I used essay prizes to overcome my writer's block by picking one essay prize that looked interesting then committing to writing and submitting an essay by the deadline **no matter what**. As a result, some of my early essays were pretty poor but I submitted them anyway. This gave me experience with the process of writing and improved my skills. I also came to accept that my essays will never be perfect and there's no way to guarantee I'll win a prize. Seth Godin advises us to "always be shipping"; to finish the work we start and share it with others.

Since overcoming my initial life-long writer's block, I've discovered a deep love of writing and have written many essays, blog posts and articles as well as this book. I appreciate not everyone will develop this depth of enjoyment but it's worth the time investment to find out. I highly recommend entering at least one essay prize while at medical school for this purpose.

2. **Improve**

Aim to learn as much as possible from everything that you write. Improving writing involves trial and error as well as learning from feedback.

Friends who will kindly proofread your work are invaluable. I also find it useful to read back my work a month or so after writing it, trying to look through the eyes of someone who has never read it before. Sometimes you will receive feedback on essay prize entries but this tends to be fairly limited. The level of 'success' of a piece of writing can be a rough indicator of its quality; whether an essay wins a prize or how many comments or views a blog post receives.

Don't be afraid to show your work to others. It can be tempting not to open up your work to the criticism of others but this feedback is essential. It can be easy to assume you have got your point across clearly because it already makes sense to you. It isn't until someone else reads it that you will know for certain.

Further resources

If you are interested in developing writing, two of the best books on this subject are:

On Writing Well by William Zinsser, which is a comprehensive breakdown of how to write good non-fiction, written with beautiful clarity (being true to itself) that is a pleasure to read and will change the way you write forever.

Bird by Bird by Anne Lammott, which considers writing from the human angle, considering the anxieties and challenges of being a writer. Although written for a fiction-writing audience, contains many lessons that hold true for writing fiction or non-fiction.

~~~

MEDICAL STUDENT CHALLENGE 3: Get at least ten hours of teaching experience.

MEDICAL STUDENT CHALLENGE 4: Enter at least one essay prize. Select a title and commit to submitting an essay no matter what.

~~~

CHAPTER 6 SUMMARY

- Effective written and oral communication helps in medicine and other areas of life.
- There are some medical conversations you won't have as a student. Developing good oral communication skills helps you adapt to this once qualified.
- Oral communication skills can be improved through talking to patients, members of the healthcare team and through teaching.
- As a medical student, writing ability can be developed through essay prizes, freelance articles, writing for scientific journals and blogging.
- The first hurdle is to get started. Improvement comes from continual trial-and-error.

Is Medicine Right For Me?

"Is medicine really for me?" is a question that a lot of medics ask at some point during their career. Perhaps you're fed up of exams, not enthusiastic about working nights and weekends for the foreseeable future, or just don't think it's a good match for your personality. Whatever your reasoning, there are a few points worth bearing in mind.

It's worth noting that whatever your source of dissatisfaction, no career change is going to immediately solve this. It's easy in a moment of frustration to think "screw this, my life would be so much easier if I became a (insert 'dream job' here). The reality is every profession will have its own upsides and downsides. Identify your fundamental sources of dissatisfaction and consider whether you can improve the situation or whether it will change in future as your career progresses.

The flip-side of this is that you mustn't feel obliged to stay in medicine for fear of leaving. Leaving medicine can seem like a daunting task, particularly if you've been on that pathway for a long time, it's what your friends and family expect, and it's such a 'safe' career path. However, staying in any job for this reason is not a source of long-term satisfaction.

Switching career involves a significant amount of work over a sustained period of time. It's easy to underestimate this, but in a lot of alternative career paths a medical degree won't count for a huge amount. You'll often need to demonstrate your merits in other ways.

The best approach to take is to **do your research**. Even if you do the research and decide to stick with medicine, you'll only feel more content in medicine for having done so. I'll help you get started and signpost to other useful resources.

Broadly, there are three routes you can take:

- **Find a clinical practice that suits you.** For example, if you desire flexibility, the "E-ROAD" specialities (ENT, radiology, ophthalmology, anaesthesiology and dermatology) allow doctors good control of their time spent working.
- **Find a non-clinical, medically-related job**, such as scientific research, medico-legal work, teaching, public health, medical communications, medical entrepreneurship and medical management consultancy.
- **Find a job unrelated to medicine**, which can be pretty much anything, although some have greater overlap of skills gained from medicine than others.

I won't explore these in depth here but there is lots of information on the internet on what each job involves and many forums discussing previous doctor's experiences of the transition.

The best resources which consider career route more broadly are:

The **80,000 hours career guide** (https://80000hours.org/career-guide/) – 80,000 hours (named after the average number of hours in a person's career) are a non-profit organisation who provide advice on career selection and have produced this excellent practical guide which can be viewed as a video series, in blog posts or as an eBook. They have also written a careers guide on Medicine from the point of view of making a positive contribution to society (https://80000hours.org/career-reviews/medical-careers/). Interestingly, its conclusions on the positive impact of clinical practice weren't as favourable as you may expect and they suggest a few other related careers which may enable larger impacts.

'Do you feel like you wasted all that training?' by Michael McLaughlin is a book that specifically addresses questions about making a career transition out of medicine. It is aimed towards a US audience but offers lots of sensible and pragmatic advice from someone who made the switch from clinical practice to medical communications quite late in his career (aged 33).

So Good They Can't Ignore You by Cal Newport is a book written for a more general audience which makes a counter-argument to the idea of "following your passion". It argues that you should work hard to develop valuable skills which will then enable you to craft a career you love.

"Don't be a donkey" (https://sivers.org/donkey) – this short blog post by Derek Sivers outlines a very useful way of thinking about careers, of particular relevance to anyone who is worried about not having enough time to all the things they want to do.

Deciding whether or not to leave clinical medicine can be a difficult decision. There's no one-size-fits-all answer and it's up to us to figure out what's best in our individual cases. The best way to enable an informed, educated decision is by a thorough exploration of ourselves and of our options.

During a period of uncertainty, it is worthwhile to develop fundamental transferrable skills. Being able to learn faster, think more clearly and communicate more effectively will help no matter what career you end up in. I hope that this book provides you with a springboard to improve these skills and create a career that you love.

<div align="center">~~~</div>

CHAPTER SUMMARY

- **You may question whether medicine is for you. Identify the source of your dissatisfaction and consider if it can be solved.**
- **Don't stay in medicine purely out of fear of the unknown.**
- **Research different career options thoroughly before making the change.**
- **Develop transferrable skills in the meantime.**

If Medicine Gets You Down

I left the ward without telling anyone and headed back to my room. I slumped down on my bed, put on some music and stared at the ceiling.

It was the fifth week of my first ever clinical placement and it wasn't going well.

I'd started out with enthusiasm. "Finally, I'll be doing what I've wanted to for years!"

But I'd found it tough. Every day, I went to the wards and wasn't really sure what I was supposed to be doing. I felt like I wasn't learning that much and that I kept getting in everyone's way.

Over time, this feeling of discomfort had become increasingly draining and the initial excitement had started to wear off. Getting out bed to head to the wards was becoming more of a challenge.

I started to wonder: Maybe I'm just not very good at this? Maybe medicine just isn't for me?

~~~

During medical school there will be times when you feel low. Sometimes there will be an obvious cause, at other times there may not be. This is part of being human.

We all have fears and hang-ups, whether we are aware of them or not, and medical school can force us to confront these. As you undergo new stressful experiences, it is important to find your own ways to cope with the trials and tribulations of life and of studying medicine. Some methods are healthier than others but what's important is that it works for you. A prominent South African trauma surgeon told me that when he is feeling down, he would take his helicopter and repeatedly take off and land while aiming for the same spot on the ground. This may sound bizarre but it worked for him.

Here are some approaches that myself and colleagues use which have been helpful. Of course, nothing that we do will guarantee eternal happiness and contentment but I share them here in the hope that they may help:

1. Make a central refuelling resource
2. Mix it up
3. Change your physical state (and your mind will follow)
4. Write your way out
5. Incorporate a new daily practice
6. Other suggestions

It's worth nothing that I'm fortunate enough to have never been seriously 'depressed' (as medically defined) but not everybody is so lucky. In fact, mental illness and suicide rates are higher amongst medical students and doctors. If you feel at any point that there's a chance you may be clinically depressed, seek professional help. You are not alone and there is a lot of support out there for you. Speak to your GP, phone a helpline or try some self-help CBT modules. And, especially, speak to someone before you do anything that will harm yourself or others, no matter how hopeless you may feel.

Make a central refuelling resource

"Dear Future Chris,

I've compiled this resource for you.

For when you feel drained of energy, disheartened or depressed, frustrated, confused or overwhelmed, with no apparent end in sight.

Use this book to give you the strength and energy to push through.

Past Chris"

This is the first message in my central refuel document that I started creating about half-way through medical school. I have continually added new content to it since then. It now contains a mix of quotes, short letters to myself, photos, thoughts, reminders of experiences to induce certain emotional states, videos, suggested actions and more. I've very much tailored it to what I know my bummed-out self will respond to.

Mine is an electronic document but friends of mine have written in notebooks or collected things in folders. Such refuelling resources can be an effective way to reconnect with yourself and remember your priorities. They can be effective for pulling you out of a low mood.

Mix it up

A lack of variation can make us feel stuck in a rut. The best solution for this is to deliberately do something we've never done before. It can be anything that breaks up the normal pattern of things.

Ask yourself 'What's one thing I could try that I've never done before?'

Maybe you want to sit in the park and read a book. Maybe you want to sign up for a dance class. Maybe you want to join a new club.

It can help if it is something outside of your comfort zone. You could go to a party where you only know one or two people. You could go out for dinner or to the cinema by yourself. You could ask that girl or guy on a date.

It can literally be anything (as long as it's legal). Be creative and be impulsive. Don't stop and rationalise, just do it.

Change your physical state (and your mind will follow)

Science has shown that our body has a massive impact on our mind. If we smile, our mind starts to assume we are happy. If we walk with a confident posture, we start to feel confident.

Two useful ways to improve your state of mind are to:

1. Get moving

If you're feeling stagnant, bored, frustrated or down for whatever reason, getting your body moving can be a great help.

Go for a walk outside. If you find motivation difficult, just focus on getting your shoes on. Then focus on getting out of the front door. With each action, your momentum will build. By the time you are home from your walk you may feel reinvigorated.

While walking, look around you. Let the beauty of the world wash over you. Take your time. Forget about the world.

Listening to music or an audiobook while you walk can help. Classical music such as Ludovico Einaudi can be relaxing.

Motivational audiobooks, such as Tony Robbins' "Unleash the Giant Within" or Brian Tracy's "Maximum Achievement", can help to get your motivation back up.

2. Take an ice-cold shower

Forcing yourself to stand under icy cold water for 30 seconds or so can have an immense 'resetting' effect on your mind and be reinvigorating. If you find it too difficult, you can gradually work up to it. It requires motivation to overcome the initial resistance to the cold water but after pushing through the initial discomfort, it can feel uplifting and sensational.

Write your way out

Writing can be a great way to process thoughts, feeling and emotions and can lift you out of a funk.

One powerful technique is a form of free writing as follows.

Open a blank document, put your hands on your keyboard, and just start writing about whatever comes to mind.

Don't allow yourself to stop. Don't correct any typos or grammatical errors. Don't let more than a second go by without one of your fingers tapping a key. It doesn't matter if you type so fast you can't read what you've written – don't try and read it back until later. Just keep going.

One thing that can happen is you finish typing a section and suddenly go "wow, I didn't realise I cared so much about that..." or "ohhh, that's what has been upsetting me".

Incorporate a new daily practice

Certain things, when done on a consistent basis, can have a dramatic improvement on your mood. The best way to achieve this consistency is to incorporate it into your daily routine.

For example, the "Five Minute Journal" is a book which prompts you every morning to write three things you are grateful for and three things that will make the day great. Then in the evening it asks you to write three amazing things that happened that day and how you could've made the day better. While it sounds simple and cheesy, it has been shown to boost both gratitude and productivity.

Other popular daily practices include goal setting (Brian Tracy recommends writing out your top ten goals from memory every morning), brainstorming (Earl Nightingale recommends naming a problem every day and thinking of twenty possible solutions) and meditation or prayer (depending on your spiritual preferences).

If unsure, trial a technique for 30 days and then decide whether you wish to continue.

Other suggestions

Pick up your phone and call a friend you haven't spoken to in a while.

Think of 10 things right now that you are grateful for.

Tim Ferriss advises having at least one evening a week in the company of three or more friends.

~~~

"Fall 99 times, rise 100"

- Japanese Proverb

~~~

CHAPTER SUMMARY

- Medicine and life can get us down. Some things that can help include making a refuelling resource, mixing things up, getting physical, free writing and new daily practices.

Memorisation Techniques

by James Hartley

Despite one's best efforts to learn everything for understanding, there can be times where you are presented with a list of names (the branches of the external carotid artery, for example) or numbers (doses of medications) and just have to memorise them. This happens less commonly than you might think, but it does happen; and when it does, it helps to have a few memory techniques ready to enhance your mental horsepower and make keeping those details in a little easier.

This section presents just four such techniques, with links to places you can learn more, starting very simple and moving to more advanced techniques (you can find many more by googling "mneumonic techniques"). You may find all or none of these useful – it varies from person to person, and in fact this section of Chris' great masterpiece was not written by him, because he did not use memory tricks to learn… so yeah, your mileage may vary.

1. Letter and word mneumonics

For example: complications of myocardial infarctions as DARTH VADER, signs of cerebellar dysfunction as DANISH and the causes as PASTRIES, and the aforementioned braches of the external carotid as Some Attractive Ladies Find Older… etc etc. You can finish that one off.

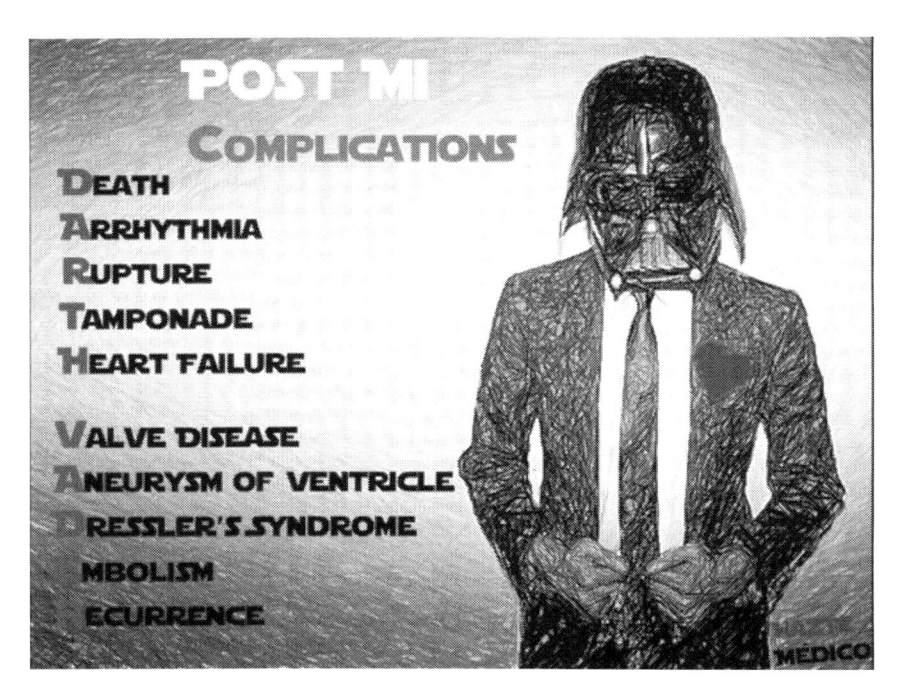

Figure 1: Star Wars - Return of the MI

Using this kind of mneumonic might seem an obvious thing, and it is – everyone uses these. However, it is worth mentioning it here for two reasons.

First, you may be unaware of just how far some people take this method of learning: for instance, , http://bit.do/mnemonics-1, http://bit.do/mnemonics-2, and even http://bit.do/mnemonics-3. Second, there are better and worse ways to use these, and better and worse mneumonics. The best mneumonics are like the ones I gave above – simple, punchy, and emotionally evocative, plus every letter stands for one and only one thing. All things which make memory *easier*, rather than just adding another layer to remember; the only missing element is being *made up by you personally*, which also aids memory. Bad mneumonics are long, boring, and redundant. This is the difference between ABCDE for assessment of a sick patient, and ABCDEFGHIJ for signs of chronic hepatitis.

Signs of chronic liver disease (ABCDEFGHIJ)

- **A**sterixis, **A**scites, **A**nkle oedema, **A**trophy of testicles
- **B**ruising
- **C**lubbing/ **C**olour change of nails (leuconychia)
- **D**upuytren's contracture
- **E**ncephalopathy / palmar **E**rythema
- **F**oetor hepaticus
- **G**ynaecomastia
- **H**epatomegaly
- **I**ncrease size of parotids
- **J**aundice

Figure 2: Increase in size of... Liver? Wait then what is the H for? Maybe it was increase in testes, I know they're in there somewhere, and I've already used A three times...

2. Method of loci and story associations

So ya'know Sherlock, where the most titular detective has his very own "Mind Palace" where he can retreat to find facts and make connections in the moments between the action? Well, this is the technique he is using! Apart from, well, a realistic version rather than some feverish invention of Steven Moffat's diseased mind. So don't expect Benedict Cumberbatch appearing in your head to teach you about pharmacology.

The real method of loci involves using the fact that our minds seem very, very good at remembering a few things very well – particularly places (think of the town you grew up, or your primary school; how much would you bet you could still find your way around a pretty large area if dropped back there, after many years. That is a lot of information you've retained with very little effort!). The idea is to, as you learn, construct in your head a place, real or imaginary, and hang pieces of information in that place as memorable events, features, or else. The resulting mental structures will be highly individual (as will the success rate of this method). An example: I have the different kind of leukaemia in a court in Vauxhall where I once lived. Further away from me are the lymphoid cancers, closer the myelogenous ones (this makes sense, as lymphoid cells are a feature of the more "advanced" adaptive immune system, so you have to move further to get to them). In the far right corner (the CLL zone), are a gaggle of old men, who start cackling at you if you go too close. This is because CLL mainly affects the old (M:F 2:1), and is actually pretty asymptomatic most of the time, so they might as well laugh … and so on. Weird, right?

A related method for ordered lists is to tie the words and concepts into a story, again making it as emotionally evocative as possible. I have one for the inhibitors of CYP450 enzymes involving giant mushrooms and being thrown up on in the subway…

Figure 3: The mushrooms represent antifungal azoles. See, not so weird, right?

I've successfully used this kind of method to remember lists of more than 20 drugs, bacteria, or similar things after only one reading and a couple of mental revisions, and, combined with the Spaced Repetition technique described above, retained them indefinitely. So, it does work, but you'll have to try it for yourself.

Some resources: https://artofmemory.com/wiki/Method_of_Loci, https://remembereverything.org/memory-palace-the-method-of-loci/, http://www.skillstoolbox.com/career-and-education-skills/learning-skills/memory-skills/mnemonics/mnemonic-systems/story-mnemonic-system/. Basically, just google the terms.

3. Major System technique

The techniques I introduce above are great for remembering words and concepts… but a lot of the time, the hardest things to remember are numbers. What proportion of this syndrome's sufferers are male? What is its mortality? What is the dose of co-amoxiclav? What is the half life of CRP?

The major system technique is a kind of add on which allows you to use the normal mnemonic methods on numbers as well, by simply converting them to words. It's pretty simple in concept – you give every digit 0-9 a consonant's sound, or range of similar sounds, as well as a meaning, and then when you need to remember a long number convert it to sounds, change the sounds to a word or phrase, and if necessary work it into a story or whatever to tie it to the concept you need it for. A simple example using my major system sounds (slightly different to the traditional sounds used by most people, for no good reason) is as follows:

Sounds

0. Z
1. T, d
2. N
3. M
4. R, l
5. V, F
6. S, Sch
7. C, K
8. G, Y
9. P, b

Which means that the image of a meteor plunging into the ocean, releasing a spurt of bright pink flame, is…

MeTeoR DiVe PiNK, which is…

31415927, which is…

More digits of pi than I'll ever need as a doctor, but what the hell, this was an example.

A more relevant example is: How much co-amoxiclav do you need? A ton. ToN: 1.2 grams TDS.

You get the picture. The key with this technique is to practise it a lot, and randomly – every time you see a number, in any art of life, try to convert it to its sounds as quickly as possible, or convert words to their numbers.

Resources to get you started: http://bit.do/memory-4, http://bit.do/memory-5, http://bit.do/memory-6.

4. Synesthetic memory

This might just be a typical mind fallacy thing, but I find concepts, numbers, whatever much easier to remember when they have colours, emotions, images etc associated with them. For example, in my head, all of the cytokines associated with Th2 immunity are blues and turquoises, Th1 tans, Cd8 immunity reds and warm colours. One and five are sharp numbers, four is a dark red square with rounded edges, 3 is orange, 2 feels a little uncomfortable. I do this automatically if I am learning something I'm interested in, but if I'm trying to learn something I'm less excited about have to do it manually, so to speak, and it helps.

Learning from others

During your medical degree, as you cycle through different rotations, you will meet some inspirational doctors. They may teach you things that stick with you for life. There are many things you can learn from an inspirational individual that you can't learn from any textbook.

Below I've collated the best and most memorable pieces of advice that I receive from doctors during my time at medical school. Everybody will meet different teachers and learn different things during their medical school experience – I hope that by the end of your time at medical school you will have your own. These points are not meant to replace what you will learn, but rather to supplement the insights that you gain.

Wisest words

Neurox, not xerox

After missing a teaching session, I emailed the consultant neurologist who had run the session asking for a summary of the supervision or some notes. His one-line email reply was the above. This simple phrase has stuck with me and helped me realise the benefit of committing things to memory rather than keeping comprehensive notes.

The first thing you prescribe to a patient is yourself

A psychiatrist explained how easy it can be to think medicine is all about what you do regarding a patient's management; what drug you prescribe or operation you recommend. However, your interaction with them can have a lasting impact so it's important to be friendly and to inspire confidence.

The power of observation

One GP emphasised how much can be gained from observation – of doctors, as both positive and negative role models, and of patients:

"Find a good role model. Observe them; what is it that they say? What is it that they do? Little things can make a huge difference. Likewise, notice doctors that make you think 'I never want to be like that'; What is it that they said and did which had a negative impact on patients?"

"With patients, observe like a detective - you can gain a huge amount from their expression, posture, gait, breathing, and other nonverbal signs. For example, you can pick up a chest problem by noticing uneven breathing or depression by the lowered gaze and the slumped posture."

Always ask why

A cardiac surgeon explained that his habit of asking why was one reason for his successful career.

"Keep asking why. Some people will get annoyed. They may realise they don't actually know why. But keep asking and you will get to the bottom of things."

Never use 'executed' when you can use 'did'

Keep it simple in the way you use your language as the purpose is to communicate a message. Don't use complicated words to sound smart as you will limit your audience. This is true when talking to your patients and when writing to share ideas.

Know the meaning of every word that you use

It is easy to use words without being sure of their meaning. A doctor told me this in a vascular clinic, after I wasn't sure exactly what an 'ulcer' is (it is the loss of epithelium).

When a patient comes to you with a 'functional' problem, it's because they have a problem which they can't deal with on their own.

Conclusion

Medical school can be tough but it can also provide some of the best times of our lives. Our approach to medical school can determine the projection that the rest of our medical career takes. In this book, I have laid out the approach that I believe a medical student in the 21st century should take. I sincerely hope that it helps you to get the most out of your medical school experience to set up a successful and fulfilling career.

I hope that Chapter 1 helps you to find that ever-elusive work-life balance and that Chapters 2 and 3 help you to excel academically while having more time for other things. I hope that Chapter 4 helps you to make an impact in medicine and, in combination with Chapters 5 and 6, helps you to find an area of passion and develop fundamental transferrable skills for whatever path your life takes.

Throughout the book, I set four 'Medical Student Challenges'. Here they are again. Give them a go and tick them off once completed.

	Completed? (Date)
Medical Student Challenge 1: Self-educate in a topic that interests you. Set a goal to work towards and a deadline for achieving it.	
Medical Student Challenge 2: Undertake at least one research project based on an idea that you come up with.	
Medical Student Challenge 3: Get at least ten hours of teaching experience.	
Medical Student Challenge 4: Enter at least one essay prize. Select a title and commit to submitting an essay no matter what.	

Epilogue

Thank you!

Thank you for reading this book. I sincerely hope that you got a lot out of it. I worked hard to make sure it would be a worthwhile read.

Tell your friends

I appreciate that not all parts of this book will appeal to all people. My aim has been to cover enough areas and different perspectives that anybody who reads the book will gain something from doing so. If you have a friend or family member who would enjoy it, please let them know about it or, better yet, buy them a copy.

A favour

Finally, if you enjoyed this book, I have one small favour to ask.

Would you be kind enough to leave a review for this book on Amazon?

I'll even give you a further incentive: E-mail the link of the review you write (to chris@medicalstudentmanual.com) and I will send you one of three private guides that I have written on (i) writing excellent academic essays, (ii) how to learn faster or (iii) how to maximise sleep efficiency. Just let me know which one.

About the Author

Chris Lovejoy (www.chrislovejoy.me) graduated in Medicine from Cambridge University in 2017.

He is passionate about education and hopes that the upcoming generations of doctors are able to adapt to the future challenges of healthcare. He's also interested by technology and its potential applications in healthcare and elsewhere.

Outside of medicine, he enjoys basketball, music and reading good books.

Printed in Great Britain
by Amazon